Green Pastures of a Barren Land:

finding contentment in life's desolate seasons

by
Candise Moody Farmer

Green Pastures of a Barren Land:
finding contentment in life's desolate seasons©
By Candise Moody Farmer

Copyright © 2012 by Candise Moody Farmer

ISBN 978-0-9826561-3-6

Library of Congress Control Number: 2012942067

Printed in the United States of America by Lightning Source, Inc.

Cover design by Jessica Anglea www.jessicaanglea.com
Text design by Debbie Patrick, Vision Run, www.visionrun.com

Free Church Press
P.O. Box 1075
Carrollton, GA 30112

Dedication

For you, Jesus –
My Savior and Friend

A Note to the Readers

Although this work details my experience with biological barrenness and childlessness, the references to the healing I obtained through God's Word are certainly applicable to every disappointing and hurtful situation. My earnest prayer is for my sweet Lord and Savior, Jesus Christ, to use the Scriptural principles outlined within this book to bring restoration to anyone who may be encountering a barren season of life.

For the reader struggling with any diverse pain or loss, may your soul be found "resting in the green pastures" of a barren land.[1] And for you, my sister, "the barren woman," may you "abide as a joyful mother of children."[2]

Candise

CONTENTS

Foreword

**from Kay Arthur,
author, speaker, and founder of Precept Ministries
International**

I am delighted to introduce you to *Green Pastures of a Barren Land* and its author, Candise Farmer. With great anticipation, I look forward to hearing of the countless lives that will be transformed by the power of God's Word, which is accurately and beautifully interpreted within this book. Candise is taking her personal experience with childlessness and infertility (which, I believe, is often an "unspoken" heartache) and is utilizing it as a ministry springboard to lead thousands of folks into a closer look at the Scriptures.

All humans are prone to plan for themselves a pleasant life. Even on a daily basis, we tend to pre-determine the outcome of our day – what we will accomplish, who we plan to see, where we expect to go. These day-to-day expectations develop into week-by-week hopes, and then these weekly aspirations lead to monthly goals. And then before we know it ... we have set before us our life's blissful agenda. We have it all planned out. Our plans may include a happy marriage, a fulfilling career, healthy children, profitable investments, and leisure golden years. And certainly, the "dreams" we have for ourselves do not include cancer, divorce, infertility, broken relationships, life-altering accidents, etc.

Disappointment, personal loss, failed plans are a universal reality; everyone will encounter some form of regret within his/her lifetime. The question then becomes ... Now what? What are we going to do now that things didn't work out as we had hoped or planned? How will we respond to the pain and defeat?

The answers are found within the book you are holding. Candise has uncovered seven principles from the Bible that are the keys to finding contentment and joy in all circumstances. She has studied the Scriptures inductively for over ten years with Precept Ministries, and now she is extending the hope of the Word to you. If your heart is breaking and your crushed dreams have left you with no hope for living, encountering this work could be your "turning point."

I encourage every believer to read this book. At some point and time, a hurtful circumstance will enter everyone's life, and the seven Bible-based truths of this work can provide complete restoration.

Preface

My dear sister, I'm assuming if you are reading this book you are a "victim," at least to some extent, of the monster of infertility or pregnancy loss. I'm assuming you are the young wife whose heart is aching for the baby you've never gotten to hold. Or maybe you're the 30-something survivor of years of loss who is now needing to accept the possibility of a childless marriage. Perhaps you're the mom of a confused, grieving daughter who now (after multiple miscarriages) is questioning every "Sunday School Bible Truth" she's ever been taught. Or maybe you're the one, the *only* one – the only woman of whom you know who will never get her baby. If this is you, my heart feels every emotion of your pain, and I want so badly to caress your sweet face in my hands, look you in the eyes and say, "I am so sorry, and I love you." There is a paranormal bond that exists between those of us women who have walked through the valley of infertility or pregnancy loss. It is a crisis we wish upon no one, and our hearts break for those dealing with the disappointment – because of this … we are sisters, joined in our innermost beings, pierced by the loss and striving simultaneously to survive.

During my twelve-year encounter with multiple miscar-riages, I saturated myself with all kinds of Christian books dealing with the complex subject of barrenness. Within those pages, I found much comfort. I read of women who had experiences much like mine; I quickly discovered that my complicated whirlwind of emotions relating to my infertility was completely normal and universal among the "league of unsuccessful procreators." Their stories com-forted me. It was healing for me to discover that I was not the only woman who had cried while walking down the baby-food aisle at the grocery store. I was not alone; other women, too, avoided Baby Dedications and Mother's Day services at church. And within one book's pages, I discovered that a hysterosalpingogram was a fairly common proce-dure, and I was assured I could handle the few moments of discomfort.

God has endowed many gifted ladies with vital minis-tries to author such books, and I cannot imagine just how lost and alone I would have been without such resources in my life. But as I read, listened, and simply exposed myself to the world of miscarriage and failed pregnancy attempts, I rarely encountered a woman who never got her baby. As I reflect back upon the sidebars in "empty cradle" books, testimonies of infertile women at ladies' conferences, miscarriage stories of a "friend-of-a-friend" and the memoirs of scores of women battling my monster, the account of the wife who, in the end, did not get her baby, wasn't the vivid story I remembered. Yes, I could detail the chapter about the husband and wife (who, after years of tests, numerous attempts at in vitro-fertilization, and several early-pregnancy miscarriages) finally got their miracle baby. I often retold myself the outcome of "Amy's" journey of infertility, which resulted in the birth of "Baby Brooke," who now has twin brothers on the way. Even after many years, I could vividly envision the little gal at the ladies' retreat who testified about her years of loss, and then concluded her message by motioning for little "Allie" to join her on stage as a testimony of God's goodness. All the stories seemed to have a happy ending; the loving couple somehow, in the end, held their miracle and lived within the blessings of parenting a life from God.

But when the clouds of grief swallowed my very existence, and I became barren forever – never to carry, birth, nurse, or nurture a child – I had no reference, no referral, no research that could accompany me to the dreaded place of finality ... never a baby, the state of incurable barrenness.

With a notion of this work's content before you, it is my speculation that you may be there ... in the excruciating reality of never getting your baby. If this is you, my prayer is for the supernatural love of God Almighty to extend through the pages of this book, miraculously wrap itself around you and restore your soul in a way that can solely be explained by the mercy of an All-Powerful God.

As you venture into this book, I encourage you to read carefully each passage from the Bible. You will find some prefacing a chapter. Some will be scattered among references to doctor's appointments and journal entries; wherever they may be found, I beg you to please read them with prayerful reflection. When reading other "empty cradle" books, I would often find myself so engrossed in the "storyline" of *Mr. and Mrs. Trying To Conceive* that I was tempted to skim over the Scripture passages in order to eagerly discover the couple's outcome – did they get their baby. Please don't make this mistake. The most crucial words of this book are those in bold font recorded straight from God's Word. They contain the principles that saved my life, and I want their healing power to gloriously affect you. So, please, vow now to earnestly consider each passage and allow His Word to minister to you.

Green Pastures of a Barren Land

Prologue: Sharing My Story

"And they overcame him by the blood of the Lamb, and by the word of their testimony ... " Rev. 12:11

I taught my first Sunday School class when I was in high school, and I've been teaching, to some capacity, ever since. Presenting His Word is the spiritual gift God handpicked for me. Just as God has gifted some to extend His mercy through homeless shelters and equipped others with the gift of discernment, He has placed upon me His call to relate to others truths from the Scriptures. Much of the time, I feel inadequate in this ministry, and I fearfully and reverently understand my responsibility.

The Bible needs no other assistance in impacting lives; the Word alone is power unto salvation and restoration.

Over the years, as I've stood before classes, clubs, and student groups, I've rarely shared from my personal experiences. I absolutely love God's Holy Word, and I know without a doubt that there is no greater power than the spoken Word of God. I've been in student services and witnessed well-known, anointed speakers simply reading the Bible and scores of teens surrendering to Christ. The Bible needs no other assistance in impacting lives; the Word alone is power unto salvation and restoration. I'm convinced of this truth, and it may be this awareness that prompted me into a tendency to see my personal stories of life as insignificant and not worthy for sharing.

In the summer of 2010, God began to deal with my heart, and through His Word I began to understand that there *can* be a vibrant ministry when Christ's followers share from their personal lives. He showed me that He could be glorified and others could receive encouragement from me telling my story. After all, God brought every happening, every particular condition, every specific moment into my life. He orchestrated it all, and surely He had planned to be glorified within each detail. Now, realizing that my testimony of infertility is a Divine tool handcrafted for me by God, I'm humbly availing it to you for healing and strength.

It was a post-Christmas family dinner at my parents' house. Just me, Rusty (my wonderful husband of 19 years), my brother, his wife, our parents, and our widowed little Granny. We had enjoyed another huge meal, lots of laughter, and chatter around the table. It was happy times for the Moody household. After we had stuffed ourselves (again), we all sat around the table amidst our "cleaned plates," almost-empty glasses, and slightly soiled napkins (some refolded, some wadded up). Jon Paul, my only sibling and five years my junior, strolled from the table over to the counter to retrieve a stack of newly developed photos from his trail camera. (For you gals with nominal outdoor/hunting backgrounds, that's an automatic camera that you hang on the base of tree and point to a wildlife feeder in hopes of getting some record of grazing trophy whitetail bucks or wild turkeys.) As he walked back to the table holding out the stack to my parents, we heard, "Hey, check out these new trail camera pictures I got today." And at that moment, my heart stopped. I knew in an instant where this was going. I didn't consciously think it through, but I felt the intensity of the moment before it impacted our worlds forever.

It was just two years earlier that I had my own stack of photos. I had just been to the doctor for an OB setup. I was a few weeks pregnant. Not a soul knew but me, Rusty and our families. At that time I was working for a family in our area, helping "school" their adorable three little girls. These little princesses were next to family for me. I worked with them five days a week, and over the course of 12 plus years, I had let them move into my heart as "almost" children of my own. My family knew I was expecting, and next to tell on my list were "the girls." For them, my having a baby would be getting a real live baby doll. Nothing would have thrilled them more than for "Miss Candise" to have a baby.

The day after my first set of ultrasound pictures I decided to let them in on the wonderful secret. I had recently had some photos developed from one of our educational outings. These new pics would serve as part of the "announcement." About halfway through the stack of the field-trip photos, I ingeniously inserted an ultrasound shot. How clever. So here the four of us sat. My heart just pounding. I was trying desperately not to let my face show the excitement. The oldest, Anne, flipped through them one by one as her little cousins peered over each of her shoulders. I knew they were getting close.

And then ... flip. There it was. They all three just stared at the tiny baby, and then as if Anne was speaking for all three of them, it was "Aww, Miss Candise." They were ecstatic! Jumping, smiling, screaming – just a moment from heaven that could annoy most dads who had already heard one-too-many "little-girl shrills."

Yet, years later, here I sat with my family at the supper table, childless still. It was as if the moment upon us was in slow motion. My dad flips one by one. Nice buck. Couple of raccoons. Mom is leaning in to note each critter caught on camera. And then WHAM! There was the "announcement" via an ultrasound picture. Yes, my little brother (who'd only been married two-and-a-half years) and his wife would be the first grandchild donors of the family. It was the most intense realization of my life. I was instantly overcome by emotion – all sorts of emotions. In a split second, but what felt to be an eternity, it was like I left my body and gazed upon the commotion with anger, disappointment, envy, disgust, broken-heartedness, regret, immense sadness, and then loneliness. It was as if I was watching a family that I no longer knew, a family which I no longer felt a part of and no longer wanted to be a part of. I felt the rug of stability and acceptance that I had been standing on for 36 years being jerked out from underneath me. And there I was. Standing where I'd never stood before. Standing alone. Critically wounded. Crippled, yet somehow still standing.

Rusty and I left the family gathering that night almost speechless. But within the few words of dialogue, we both agreed we had seen it coming. We had seen it coming but had not prepared ourselves for it. The few days after our family's pregnancy party (as I soon labeled the event in my own mind) marked the beginning of my journey to the pit of barrenness. Emotions that I had never encountered began to overtake me.

The complexity of emotions. If you have spent any time at all on the road marked by infertility, you know fully what I'm talking about. How can any circumstance lead to such intense, unexplainable, and complicated emotions? A simple medical condition (as some people see it) of not being able to conceive, incubate and then birth a healthy life can become a spark that ignites the most complicated situation of your entire existence. You know what I'm talking about. You may be in the pit now. Or perhaps you feel as if you're sliding down its side, grasping for all you're worth at every rationale. Wherever you are in your state of infertility and/or pregnancy loss, please know that the vast gamut of emotions that seems to be imprisoning you is normal. You are not alone. To some extent, we've all been there. The sisterhood (which you may or may not know to exist) is with you on this. Your anger, your doubt, your fear, your grief, your disappointment … it is all common to the condition. It characterizes every case. Whether the plague of unannounced and uncontrollable emotion is at Stage Four or at an early detection phase, all women who've encountered infertility have at some point become subjected to these all-too-common symptoms.

My lowest point came quickly after the post-Christmas pregnancy announcement. At this point, I had gone through three miscarriages, endless batteries of tests (including extensive genetic research, two hysterosonograms, a laparoscopic hysteroscopy, Factor IV testing), three D & C's and a myomectomy (fibroid removal). I had seen, as my general OB-GYN had labeled, the "best infertility-endo-crinologist specialist in our part of the country." I drove over two hours to see a high-risk obstetrician during my third pregnancy (to little avail). And I was even sent to a hematologist-oncologist for an enormous blood workup to make sure I didn't have a clotting disorder that would have caused the "habitual abortions." (To this day, I despise that misleading medical term!) And all of this "trying to have a baby" effort had taken place within eight short years. I was wiped out! Tired of the effort, tired of the failure, tired of the fear, tired of the discussion. I was tired of living with the fact that I had been married fourteen years, was approaching thirty-five years old, and was still looking at a future with no children.

I started on an emotional and spiritual nosedive. I was unaware of how to cope with the pain. We lived in a small rural town, and we attended a small rural church. I knew of no one who had encountered infertility in the way I had. Yes, I knew of a couple of older ladies in town who had battled up to four miscarriages before filling their family nests, but there was absolutely no one in my life (apart from a precious lady who lived on the other side of the state) who could relate to me and possibly help me trudge through this excruciating valley. My church did not have a "Ladies in Waiting" group that met on Tuesday mornings to study the Biblical account of Hannah. I was completely alone in this darkness, with no one to help me save myself. And the scariest part was no one knew I needed saving.

Deliverance. Recovery. Wholeness. Health. How did I get here? How was I ever able to escape the despair of my barrenness? How today, after yet another miscarriage, has my life been restored? How have I been able to cope with the finality of a hysterectomy? This is what I hope to reveal to you, precious reader. There is hope. Over the course of my recovery, God revealed to me seven principles from His Holy Word that literally saved my life.

I never thought I'd be able to survive a life that ended in childlessness, much less survive with peace, contentment and hope. During the years of fertility treatment, I would occasionally lose control of my thoughts and begin to envision "the end." Those moments of imagining a day when a diagnosis would leave me barren forever would literally traumatize me. I shook with thoughts of never carrying a baby to full term, never getting to change the guest room into a nursery, never getting to see our child sing in the Christmas program, never getting to stand with all the mothers for applause during the Mother's Day service at church, never having a "Girls' Day" shopping outing with my adult daughter and her daughter. Those possibilities seemed hopeless and torturous to me. I had often projected that if I had to finish my life with all of these "nevers" as a reality, I would also *never* make it through. And I surely wouldn't *want* to make it through either.

> I never thought I'd be able to survive a life that ended in childlessness, much less survive with peace, contentment and hope.

But, I'm standing here on the "other side" now. I made it! And I'm living through those "nevers" with a "peace that passes all understanding" (Philippians 4:7). And you, my sweet friend, can too. Please forgive my "school teacher" format and tendency, but I want to present these seven, life-saving principles in a somewhat structured fashion. I have dedicated a chapter to each one. I'm asking you to read and reflect prayerfully upon your emotional and spiritual condition. How have I been able to live contentedly in my condition of incurable barrenness? The answers are detailed in the following chapters. I encountered each one of these "ah ha" concepts in a life-revolutionizing reality.

They truly are "my keys" that have unlocked doors that have led me to a renewed fellowship with the Lord and a passion for a life certainly worth living – and enjoying. My earnest prayer is for them to impact you miraculously and provide you with the grace you need for your condition as a hopeful mother-to-be.

Chapter I
A Tough Pill to Swallow

Why? Why me? How on earth could I have miscarried *again?* With my first miscarriage, everyone just chalked it up as a very common occurrence that more women than you know of experience especially with the first pregnancy. After all, some research suggests that twenty-five percent of women who conceive experience a first-trimester miscarriage.[1] I was told time and time again that it was just God's way of taking care of a highly deformed and handicapped fetus; countless women miscarry, and next time would be better. With this being our first loss, I didn't pursue any testing for myself or the baby. Testing wasn't even mentioned. As explained to me, the loss was due to bad implantation. The baby appeared healthy in all respects, but the faulty implantation seemed to push him/her away from the conduit of nutrients, making prenatal survival impossible. D & C #1.

Three years later, an unexpected pregnancy also ended in miscarriage. With this loss, embryo testing was recommended. A rare genetic disorder known as Trisomy 15 was determined. This time the baby was not okay. The genetic workup revealed that *he* had one extra, fifteenth chromosome. Over the phone, my nurse explained he would not have survived even if carried to term and delivered. I remember her exact words ... "major organ damage." D & C #2 followed.

Third time's a charm? Really? Not so. Testing revealed another boy, yet "unviable" as an ablighted ovum. I was seeing a high-risk specialist at this point. He explained it was the most common form of pregnancy loss. D & C #3.

So that's three miscarriages. All completely different. All without explanation. No stone had been left unturned. I'd been investigated from head to toe. Regardless the clinic, treatment center, specialist, all tests would come back *normal*. With each test result, my family would rejoice when we were told all possibilities of disease, abnormalities, and genetic disorders were eliminated. We'd thank God for the gracious reports, but the *big question* – Why can't I have a baby? – was being left unanswered.

After our third loss and as the bellies of my sisters-in-law (Did I mention my other sister-in-law on Rusty's side of the family was pregnant too?) continued to grow, my *big question* was transformed from a medical mystery into a spiritual issue.

❧

I was on my way to destruction. I cried nonstop. More than anything, I wanted to get in the bed, pull the blinds, hide beneath the covers, and stay there forever. I had no desire to go anywhere, hated the thought of going to church, and became nauseated with thoughts of attending family events. I would beg Rusty relentlessly to let us move. I was absolutely miserable. I wanted it all to end.

As shovelfuls of emotions began to bury me alive, I started to believe – it all had to go away, or I had to go away!

I knew I was dying spiritually, emotionally, relationally and, therefore, physically. I had made attempts to save myself, but honest to goodness, I had no idea how to save myself. I'd recall little spiritual insights I had picked up over the years, and I'd attempt to saturate myself with their truths. But I found myself to be so weak, so depleted of my normal "go get 'em" nature, that I realized, *alone* I would slowly lose my life. In my deteriorating condition, God somehow miraculously helped me see the destructive, inevitable end awaiting me. And although my ability to recognize a detour from its path of hopelessness was clouded by my spiritual and emotional frailness, somehow, by God's grace, He helped me take a tiny baby step in the right direction that ultimately saved my life!

My friend, Rebecca, (whom I referenced earlier as my sole confidant who lived on the other side of the state) recommended I get some kind of help. She didn't have to convince me of the need; I was well aware of my failing and fading existence. With miles separating us, there was only so much she could do as a minister from the Lord. My very survival depended upon one phone call. In total surrender, desperation, and humility (humiliation is much more accurate), I sought an appointment with a Godly man and his wife who would become my Biblical counselors for the following months. Rebecca and I had talked about our bit of skepticism; it was going to be tough for this former Marine (by the way, I hear there is no *former* Marine) who had recently become a certified counselor and his little wife to help me. We rationalized: "After all, he is not a woman, he's never struggled with infertility, and they have two kids." But I had nowhere else to turn, and I was willing to risk my dignity (the little I had left) to admit to someone I needed a lifeline!

I thank my Sweet Savior, Jesus Christ, for escorting me into our local Biblical counseling center. On May 9, 2006, the Lord Jesus sat me down across the desk from a man and woman who used God's Holy Word to strengthen me on my recovery to "life and life more abundantly" (John 10:10). God had some tough pills for me to swallow, but upon their ingestion, my destiny was redirected.

> It was not the words or abilities of my beloved counselors that brought me life; it was the inerrant, all-sufficient Word of God that rescued my perishing soul. Within the pages of God's Holy Book, you will find all the answers to life's questions.

"Why couldn't *I* have a baby?" "Why did *I* have three miscarriages?" Although many other issues had surfaced at this point and needed to be addressed, the "Why?" question had to be answered. Please let me insert a sidebar, precious lady, and assure you of this one truth: No matter what you are facing, the Holy Bible has the answer. It was not the words or abilities of my beloved counselors that brought me life; it was the inerrant, all-sufficient Word of God that rescued my perishing soul. Within the pages of God's Holy Book, you will find all the answers to life's questions. Healing, direction, and restoration are outlined for us in God's redemptive love letter for all mankind. And upon my first encounter with Biblical counseling, I received His Word of Life for my heartbreak and confusion.

Regardless of your current fertility status (or lack thereof), you have surely asked the "why" question. You may not have verbalized your bewilderment, and you may not have allowed yourself to consciously *think through* all of your confusion. But more than likely, at the depth of your being, you have wondered why you have struggled with procreation. I am sure, to some extent, a discussion of your barrenness has entertained your thoughts: "After all, bringing another life into this world is 'the norm.' Women have babies all the time – and have for centuries. With approximately 6.989 billion folks on the planet, reproduction is no big deal.[2] So what's the problem here?" And yes, many times we discover the medical or biological answer to our question ... It may be polycystic ovarian disease, maybe it's anti-phospholipid syndrome, or perhaps a low sperm count. With the giant advances in infertility diagnosis and treatment, rarely does a woman *not* have a convincing rationale presented to her as to why she is medically labeled infertile. But even with a legitimate biological explanation, the ultimate question still surfaces: "*Why* can *I* not have a baby?"

For me, this question had to be answered. My spiritual enemy and fleshly thought processes presented me with many rationales. And still to this day, I have to monitor the dialogue that takes place within my head and combat the Adversary when his arrows are targeted my way. You've been there too: "Maybe God knew I would be a horrible mother? Maybe my husband and I would disagree about parenting styles, fight over the issue and thus succumb to divorce? Maybe this is God's judgment for my sinful past? Maybe I would have been stricken with such a severe case of post-partum that my 'sanity and stability' would have been questioned by my church friends?" The list goes on ... Sounding all too familiar? I was plagued with the "why" inquiry and needed its answer. In order for me to accept my barrenness and begin to live again, I *had* to acquire (and ultimately swallow) an explanation. And you, too, my friend, need your question answered.

I had been a student of God's Word for years. I knew the stories. (Note: *Stories* can be a misleading term for the events of the Bible. We often associate *stories* with fantasy and make-believe. *Accounts* or *events* work much better for me.) Scripture had time and time again rescued me from doubt, fear, insecurity, and heartbreak. God had always given me Scriptures for certain landmarks of life. When my first *real* boyfriend dumped me for the older, thinner gal at church, it was **Proverbs 3:5-6: "Trust in the Lord with all thine heart; and lean not unto thine own understanding. In all thy ways acknowledge Him, and He shall direct thy paths."** When I had to run 3 miles in less than 24 minutes to qualify for the basketball team, it was **Philippians 4:13: "I can do all things through Christ which strengtheneth me."** When my dear grandfather passed away, it was **Psalms 30:5: "... Weeping may endure for a night, but joy cometh in the morning."** Whenever hard times came, I knew where to turn, and I knew *what* to turn – the pages of God's Word. However, at the abyss of my loss and fertility struggle, I was almost delusional. I was so weak and worn that my attempts to hoist myself upon the lifeboat of Scripture proved futile. I couldn't fight the mind battles, and my search for the one Biblical truth that could empower me to survival and recovery seemed to be, somehow, beyond my reach.

But – there was a beginning. A beginning to my healing. And there is for you, as well. There are many actualizations that must be consumed along the path of restoration. In order for me to live a fulfilled life while "never getting my baby," I had to (and currently have to) encompass my existence around the seven Biblical truths outlined in this work. But, for me, the *inception* of my restored life began with the Great Physician's hand extending to me a tough pill to swallow. And now, beloved lady, the same life-transforming hope is being outstretched to you within the nail-scarred palm of the Savior. This is *your* beginning to healing. However, a warning is being issued. As with so many pharmaceutical treatments, your exposure to the content of the following pages may come with a temporary bit of discomfort. As you partake of what could be your life's healing remedy, please determine now to deny any urges to resist or terminate your journey of recovery that can come through God's Word. A mild, unpleasant "taste" may accompany your initial contact with the following principle, but under no circumstances, should you ever quit the curing plan. A miraculous restoration of your very life rests upon your soul's ingestion of Principle One.

Green Pastures of a Barren Land

Chapter II

Principle One: LIFE IS FROM GOD (And barrenness is too). Ouch!

Life being from God is a foundational truth that the Christian community promotes in endless efforts. We see it all the time within the pro-life campaign. Countless Scriptures declare God as the giver of life. As believers, we have a well-stocked arsenal of Biblical evidence crediting God as the Creator of each new life. Even pagans encounter difficulty when trying to explain the intricate fertilization process, the complex genetic progression of an embryo, the detailed development of a baby intrauterine, and the remarkable birthing process apart from the involvement of a *higher power*. It cannot be denied, with or without the verification of Scripture, God is responsible for each human life. But *God* involved in infertility? *God* involved in *my* infertility? What about actually *responsible* for it? Now that's tough.

Look with me into the insight from Scripture:

- In **Judges 13:3**, the angel of the Lord announces to the wife of Manoah, **"Behold now, you are barren and have no children, but you shall conceive and give birth to a son."**[1]

- Then the Lord uses Isaiah the prophet to comfort His people, and although, His reference is figurative, in the following case, we still see His involvement in reproduction: **Isaiah 66:9** states, **"Shall I bring to the birth, and not cause to bring forth? saith the Lord: shall I cause to bring forth, and shut the womb? saith the Lord."**

- In **I Samuel 1:5**, it is recorded, **"but to Hannah he (Peninnah) would give a double portion, for he loved Hannah, but the Lord had closed her womb."**[2] (Parenthetical is mine.)

- In **Genesis 16:2**, we read, **"So Sarai said to Abram, 'Now behold, the Lord has prevented me from bearing children. ...'"**[3]

- **Genesis 20:18** explains the king of Gerar's childlessness: **"For the LORD had closed fast all the wombs of the household of Abimelech."**[4]

- And a heated discussion between Jacob and Rachel reveals the source of barrenness as the frustrated husband says, **"Am I in the place of God, who has withheld from you the fruit of your womb?" (Genesis 30:2)**[5]

Our loving Father has made it very clear; life is from God, and barrenness is too. Have our modern day churches, pastors, authors, and teachers presented us with a half-truth? Perhaps in efforts to persuade people to come to Christ, the true nature of God has been misrepresented? Certainly, He is the gracious Source of all health, blessing, and life, but He is also the Sovereign Lord whose infinite ways may include hardship, sickness, and physical death. Ponder His self-description found in **Deuteronomy 32:39: "See now that I, I am He, And there is no god besides Me; It is I who put to death and give life. I have wounded and it is I who heal, And there**

is no one who can deliver from My hand."[6] It is such a profound truth. According to Scripture, our merciful "Abba, Father" (Galatians 4:6) not only is the author of life and healing, but He is also the grantor of wounds and death. He is the wondrous God of the Ages who lavishes His immeasurable love upon mankind with the birth of every child, yet He is also the unfathomable Sovereign Creator who orchestrates every minute detail of His children's lives. For you and me – the issue at hand would be childlessness, an inability to get pregnant, pregnancy loss or any form of infertility.

I wish so badly I had been required to memorize a verse or two like **Lamentations 3:37 and 38** when I was in elementary Bible drills. **"Who is there who speaks and it comes to pass, Unless the Lord has commanded it? Is it not from the mouth of the Most High that both good and ill go forth?"**[7] I had sat under teaching that convinced me all events of my life were sifted through the fingers of God, and I never doubted that God had to give permission for anything to befall me (whether good or bad). But as the battle for my life as a heartbroken "habitual aborter" began to rage, such weighty truths relating to God's sovereignty seemed to disappear from my "bank" of spiritual thoughts.

Praise the Lord for revealing to me His truth. At just the right moment, just in the nick of time, God's Holy Spirit brought comfort to my weary soul. It was an immense burden lifted, a breath of fresh air, a sense of easiness that overcame me when I realized *my barrenness was from the Lord*. And sweet sister, yours is too. **"But our God is in the heavens; He does whatever He pleases" (Psalm 115:3).**[8] Faithful Job told the Lord, **"I know that You can do all things, and that no purpose of Yours can be thwarted" (Job. 42:2).**[9] And the Biblical poster child for infertility, Hannah, accounts in the book named after

33

As a Master Artist, God is painting the canvas of your life.

her miracle child, **"The LORD kills and makes alive. ..."** **(I Samuel 2:6).**[10] Take that in, my struggling friend. Allow the Holy Spirit of God to gently penetrate that truth into your restless soul. The Lord God Almighty, the Creator and Sustainer of the Universe, the Heavenly Father who loves you more than you can imagine has brought your barrenness to you. Please don't allow the forces of evil and carnality to twist this truth within your heart and make you bitter (perhaps more bitter). Choose to embrace God's involvement in your fertility hardship.

As a Master Artist, God is painting the canvas of your life. With careful, skillful scrutiny He is deliberating upon each shade of color, hand-selecting each grade of brush, and precisely contemplating the placement of each stroke. And for you (and me), His Divine masterpiece involves your (and my) past, present, and future condition of bearing children. So there you have it, hopeful one. Life *is* from God, and barrenness is too. Embrace that. It can set you free. What comfort and healing there is in knowing your canvas of life rests upon the Master Painter's easel.

Principle One: Life is from God (and barrenness is too).

Chapter III

So, God Did This. But Why?

My healing began when I started to understand that God had allowed my three miscarriages, and ultimately, He *meant* or intended for each loss to be a part of my life. This God – that I then began to see as the agent of my losses – was no stranger to me. There was a sweet familiarity between the two of us. I had "walked" with Him some 20 plus years, and in a sense, I felt I knew the Father and He knew me. A lot of water had passed under our "Father-Daughter" bridge. I completely acknowledge that I had not spent as much time as I should have seeking to understand Him and to have fellowship with Him over the years, but I still had enough experiences with the Lord to know that He loved me. So when I began attempting to wrap my spiritual mind around the reality of His involvement in our losses, my confidence in His nature brought a sense of security to me.

Now, I know that my experience may be completely different from yours. Your journey with the Lord may not have started when you were in grade school. Your spiritual background may not include attending Vacation

Bible School as a youngster. It is very possible that you
didn't begin your walk with the Lord until just recently,
and perhaps you know very little about your Creator. If
this is you and you consider yourself to be an infant – just
recently born into the Kingdom of God – then I rejoice
with you! How wonderful! These days are so precious for
you. The newness of your life in Christ is becoming a reality.
God has chosen you, and you have accepted His invitation of forgiveness and an eternal friendship. Praise be to
God! Enjoy your early days of discovering who He is and
who you are in Him. You'll never regret surrendering to
Him and becoming His follower. If you feel your knowledge of Him is a bit shallow and uncertain, just hang on
for the ride. As you daily converse with Him, savor the
passages of His Word and seek to know Him, you will be
overcome with Him, His nature – with simply Him. For
He is Wonderful!

I also know that in reading this book, you may have
never encountered the saving grace of God. This idea of
being forgiven by a God who's responsible for all existence
and then surrendering to His lordship may be a foreign
concept to you. Or it could be that God's salvation is a gift
that you simply have refused for some time. Whatever
your situation (whether you've never understood how a
person can enter into a relationship with God or whether
the God stuff just hasn't been for you), *today* is the day
for you to begin a daily fellowship with Him. Trust me,
dear friend. If you have not confessed and repented of
your sinfulness before the Lord, recognized the penalty
for your sins and accepted God's gift of salvation made
available by the torturous murder of His only Son, then
that consideration should be your top priority for the
moment. You need the Lord. You need His forgiveness.
You need Him now, and you'll certainly need Him when
your afterlife begins. Your condition of infertility (and all

it encompasses) is a minor issue of life in comparison to your eternal destiny. You will not be able to have any real, lasting therapy or treatment apart from you first coming to know Jesus Christ as your personal Lord and Savior. So, my friend, I beg you now. If you know you do not have a saving relationship with the Lord, or if you are uncertain of His salvation upon your life, please come to the Lord right now. My greatest prayer is for you to have Christ in your life as your Savior and Lord, and I have presented God's plan of salvation in the Appendix. Please, I urge you with all that I am. Turn now to the Appendix, and allow the Lord to adopt you into His family.

So — there are the possibilities: your journey with the Lord may have just begun recently, within the past few years or months. Or perhaps, Praise the Lord, if ... you just visited the Appendix, accepted His saving gift and just within the past few minutes became born into the Kingdom of God.

> You will not be able to have any real, lasting therapy or treatment apart from you first coming to know Jesus Christ as your personal Lord and Savior.

It could be your spiritual condition is similar to mine, and it involves a somewhat long-term history of you knowing Him. Any of these circumstances could be yours.

Whatever your spiritual history may be, you've now found yourself in the midst of dealing with your barrenness. And you've just become aware that your barrenness is from this God whom you are currently beginning to know and understand or with whom you've been in fellowship for some time. At this point, your heart is probably asking, "So why? Why did He do this to me?"

That was my progression. Scripture after Scripture led me to know without any doubt that God had destined my barrenness. Step one. Then the "but why?" stone had to be overturned. Just as I had allowed the Scriptures to start my healing process, I had to rely upon them again. It was within the pages of my Creator's Love Letter to me that I found another miracle balm that soothed my wounds ... my wounds of a life lived without my babies.

So delve with me into His precepts that are able to restore your health and very life. Look with me at the answers to the "why" question. "Why has God never opened your womb and allowed you to get pregnant?" "Why has God not allowed you to birth that tiny baby whose heartbeat you watched flicker on the ultrasound screen?" "Why did God bring the rain of infertility to your household?" Brace yourself, beloved friend. Your healing has begun. Continue on your regimen of recovery — all prescribed by the Master Healer.

Chapter IV

Principle Two: <u>The Question at Hand</u>: Why Did God Do This?

<u>The Answer at Heart</u>: *For His Glory* and For My Good

I'll never forget the eye-opening moments I had with the Lord as I encountered the Biblical explanation for God allowing the pain of pregnancy loss to invade my marriage and my very existence. I had to frequently ponder the Scriptural fundamentals, pray over them and let them penetrate my heart before they completely came to life within my soul; however, my initial exposure to these truths was like a spiritual sip of a Café Mocha that felt really good going down. And now I am claiming that initial refreshment for you, as well. There is comfort during your affliction; God's Word is able to revive you (Psalm 119:50).

Explanations. Spiritual explanations. Everyone tries to offer them. With each of my four pregnancies, there came bed rest. Somehow, trouble was always detected, and my "grandfather-like" doctor would encourage me to take it easy. And on a couple of occasions, he prescribed the dreaded *total bed rest*. But in the end, I was always out-of-pocket for several weeks each time I got pregnant. I'd have to miss work, skip church, and cancel appointments in an effort to take care of that little one inside me. There would be weeks at a time that the only people who saw me were the folks who dropped by to visit, my immediate family, and doctors and nurses. As my belly grew, my once semi-stylish hairstyle would grow out. By the time I was permitted to re-enter civilization, which was always after a miscarriage and D & C, people all around me seemed to have conjured up their explanation of why I had lost another baby.

I always dreaded going back into the real world after one of my bed rest episodes. I had been on prayer lists all over the country; people who I had never met had prayed for me. And then after each loss, I'd have to get up out of the bed, try to make myself look presentable and go face those folks whose prayers seemed to have gone unanswered. Now please don't get me wrong. I love the body of Christ! Truly the universal *church* **is** beautiful! I'm amazed by God's grace each time I encounter the design and function of Christ's church. Just consider all of the believers in your life. There are countless folks, from all walks of life, united into a Divine entity as a result of Christ's sacrifice. Amazing!

However … certain *members* of Christ's body really struggle when it comes to verbally edifying a young woman who is returning to her community after losing a baby. (How'd I do? Didn't that sound nice? They *struggle*? Frankly, and more accurately stated, their explanations of "why it didn't all work out" STINK!)

I've heard it all, and I'm sure you have too. "Well, this one was probably messed up, and you wouldn't have wanted it *like that*?" "You know," they say, "you probably needed a good cleaning out. It's probably good it happened like it did and you had that D & C. Now the next one will be perfect." "You *are* a mother to so many other children at church. The Lord may just want you to take care of all of them." Or then it may be some medical explanation, such as, "It was genetics; the chromosomes didn't line up, and your baby could have never survived." This list goes on. We hear explanations that are just flat out wrong, some are speculated with little supporting evidences, some are accurate (in a sense), but for the most part, I believe the majority of them are well intended and offered as a source of reassurance.

I'll never forget "the letter." It was a few weeks after another miscarriage when *it* came. How can something as simple as going to the mailbox, getting out the mail, opening an envelope and reading a letter disrupt a home in such an outrageous fashion? My innocent, routine, daily walk to the mailbox ignited an emotional explosion that led me into a night of emotional trauma. Upon me opening and reading one of those well-intended miscarriage explanations, I fell to pieces. It seemed as if this fifty-something lady in our community had instituted "The Barren Woman's Club," and her letter was my invitation to join. I lay in the bathtub that night as Rusty walked the hall from bedroom to bedroom, and I wailed, "I don't want to be in her barren woman's club! I don't want to end up like her!" That poor lady. She'll never know the outcome of her attempt to offer an encouraging explanation. (That is unless she reads this book.) I'm sure she was trying to obey the Father, and I appreciate her heart of ministry. But I wasn't ready for its intended purpose – at the time.

Over the years, I've received these explanations. Some were offered verbally. Some issued in the form of letters and cards. Some of them brought me comfort, and some did not. Many people offered their insight as to the reason for my losses, but it wasn't until I discovered the *heavenly* explanation that healing came. When I began to consider a Biblical explanation for God allowing (or may I say *causing*?) my losses, a true, lasting comfort began to overtake my very being. *His* answer is the one I hold to everyday of my life.

Please grasp the "Part A" of this explanation and cling to it for all your worth: God sent your infertile condition (whatever it may be) and/or your history of pregnancy loss into your life *for His Glory.* In the book of John, we are introduced to a man who had been blind his entire life. (For those of us whom God has graciously endowed the gift of sight, being born into a world of darkness is a state we cannot fully comprehend.) The faint melodies of awaking songbirds and the sensation of gradually warming sunlight morning after morning may have introduced this young man to his world of blindness. And then imagine with me the hush of the village and stillness around about him coaxing him to sleep each night. Within a few hours, the cycle would continue; some smell, some sound, some stimuli would escort him into a new day of darkness and then another night of darkness. This routine of living was all he knew, all he had ever known. And I can venture to say – after years of adapting to his blindness – the notion of his sight ever being restored was rarely, if ever, considered.

John Chapter 9 states that Jesus was passing by when he saw this blind man. Obviously His disciples were with Him, being that a dialogue of the disciples' all-too-common inquisition is recorded. Perhaps the setting was a busy village street crowded with vendors of fresh produce, merchants of fabrics, and scores of folks striving to maneuver through the sea of busyness. Or it could have been a quiet scene. Maybe a simple stoned path weaving its way through insignificant, quaint dwellings scattered along a hillside. Whatever the scenario, this blind man caught the eye of Jesus and His "World Changers-in-Training."

The Scripture states the disciples asked Jesus a question upon recognizing the man's blindness: **"Master, who did sin, this man, or his parents, that he was born blind?"** (vs. 2) Wow! What a tendency of all mankind. We encounter this mind-set within the church and outside the church. Many people instantly correlate any hardship, sickness, or trial to Divine judgment brought upon the afflicted as a result of some sin.

How often do we do this with our battles of infertility? How often do we (or those around us) view our infertility as a result of some sin? It seems to be human nature. As we try to rationalize our infertile history, our thoughts tend to become manipulated. We begin to link a variety of personal sins to our condition. We do this to ourselves, and then we encounter this same tendency from others. Now, we all know from eighth-grade sex education class that there are certain forms of promiscuity that have medical consequences, and surely some cases of barrenness have been medically linked to an immoral lifestyle (or just a few moments of poor judgment). But, perhaps, we need reminding – not all infertility is a product of personal sin. Absolutely, I am aware that all sicknesses, diseases, and hardships *are* a direct result of humanity living in a fallen world, which has been plagued by sin and its consequences since Adam and Eve's initial sin in the garden. But when trials come to a believer's life, they are not always in the form of judgment. If you ever feel society's eye of judgment glaring upon you, please recognize the spiritual ignorance behind that opinion.

As noted earlier, I've taught 9th – 12th grade girls' Sunday School (now recognized as "Life Group") for years. As I have prepared for lessons – especially those related to the sanctity of human life and sexual purity – I have found within the pages of the suggested teacher's guide, statistics and medical data linking sexual impurity to infertility. These findings definitely need to be shared, but as I've stood before my class, which is aware of my unsuccessful pregnancies, there has been a bit of apprehension on my part in sharing such facts. At times, I wanted to put both fists on my hips, look those gals in the eyes and say, "OK. I do not have gonorrhea, and I've never had an abortion!" But the truth of the matter is, my dear friend, regardless of my past, your past – whether it is morally spotless or indelibly stained, as it may seem – there is complete cleansing and forgiveness through Jesus Christ our Lord. We live day to day with scars from various sins, but that is what they are – scars – totally healed over, now just a bit pink with new, soft skin, and only visible to us. We glance at them every now and then and look up with a smile, understanding what it means to live each day in the mercy and forgiveness of our Father. They remind us where we've been, and where, by His grace, we'll never walk again. Jesus is the **"Lamb of God who takes away the sin of the world."** That's my sins. Your sins. Gone ... forever **(John 1:29)**.[1] Guard yourself against any distorted mind-set. Trials and tragedy, including

> We live day to day with scars ... We glance at them every now and then and look up with a smile, understanding what it means to live each day in the mercy and forgiveness of our Father. They remind us where we've been, and where, by His grace, we'll never walk again.

infertility, are not always indicators of unconfessed sin in a believer's life.

Now return with me to the John Chapter 9 setting. Isn't Jesus so very gracious? Let's look at His response to the disciples' inference. The inquisitive followers assumed the blind man's inability to see was somehow a result of sin - either his or his parents' sin. Scripture doesn't specifically detail Christ's reaction, but I can imagine His tenderness as He took advantage of the teachable moment. Can't you envision the scene? His voice was one of patience – not frustration – and from His eyes surely flowed compassion ... compassion for these devoted followers who so desperately wanted to inhabit the mind of Christ yet daily combated fleshly thinking.

The question had been asked. Had the God who "fearfully and wonderfully" formed this man within his mother's womb been backed into a corner?[2] Someone dared to ask. Why was he born this way? Every spiritual particle and eternal being of the universe stood with perked ears and raised eyebrows.

The voice of the omniscient God of the Ages could be heard. Jesus' teaching objective was embedded in His response: **"Neither hath this man sinned, nor his parents; but that the works of God should be made manifest in him." (John 9:3)** The disciples wanted their answer, and they got their answer. Why was he born blind? Why was this poor man having to crouch against the dust-covered edging of a worn foot-path? Why was his brow furrowed with wrinkles caused by years of confusion? Why did he have to spend every moment of every day extending his sun-damaged, emaciated hand to a parade of passersby who had little time for benevolent ministries? Why was his world one of total darkness? Why was he born blind?

So "the works of God should be made manifest in him."
(John 9:3)

The phrase the *works of God* in this passage comes from the Greek word *ergon,* which implies the toilings of the Lord, acts of His effort, labors of the Father.[3] The verb of the passage, *manifest,* has a rich meaning as well. Its origin, *phaneroo,* means "to render apparent, to declare, to show forth."[4] When we dissect His simple answer, we begin to understand Christ's explanation for this man's blindness. Simply stated, he was blind **for God's glory**. This gentleman was born blind in order for God's works, His toiling and His laboring, to be shown forth and declared.

Think about that for a moment. God had a reason for bringing blindness into this man's existence. His blindness wasn't an oversight. It wasn't a "fault in production." It wasn't a judgment for sin. Instead, his blindness was issued with a predetermined, supernatural, magnificent outcome in mind. God's plan was for this man's blindness to be the source that enabled generations to fully see the hard work of God. Yes, the nameless blind man mentioned in our Bibles was a Divine conduit, serving as a spiritual passageway, by which all humanity can see the greatness of God. Through him, through his blindness, through his daily encounter with darkness, the people around him could see Light. The Divine intent of his blindness was for God to be glorified. As a result of him being born blind, his parents, his extended family, his neighbors, the little boys who played ball in the alley, the lady selling spices at the street's curb, the sisters who daily drew water from the village well were all able to witness the acts of God.

Imagine with me some "could have beens" related to this young man's story. Take a moment to see his life – a man, blind from birth. Envision his parents watching in awe as their four-year-old son mastered lacing his sandals. Mentally visit with me what his 13th birthday party could have looked like. Did you notice his uncle wiping modest tears as the visually disabled "birthday boy" quoted the entire Shema? Speculate what could have happened when (for maybe a dozen days or so) his blindness almost got the best of him. Yet with courage and Yahweh's steadfastness, the sight-impaired youngster ventured to the street again to seek a charitable coin or two. And the red-headed lad with a rag ball in hand – do you see the two comrades now? What began as episodes of insults and mockery has now been transformed into side-by-side chats over a broken bun and a few figs. And have you noticed? The business at the spice stand has been a bit slow lately. After the sightless beggar shared the Red Sea account, the lady vendor just can't get enough. Now she's spotted day after day sitting with her blind companion wanting to hear it all again ... the battle at Jericho, the slaughter of the taunting giant and countless excerpts from Christ's recent sermons. Toils, labors, acts of God made apparent and declared for all to see. The disciples surely had their answer: He was born blind **for God's glory.**

Are you seeing the connection, hopeful one? Is your spirit being restored? The Lord has an intended outcome for your walk through the valley of infertility. Your futile IVF attempts, your monthly disappointments of "still not pregnant," your traumatic miscarriage at 13 weeks, your unsuccessful commitment to bed rest, your polycystic fibrosis – your entire state of barrenness, infertility, and pregnancy loss have been prescribed to you by your Maker for a purpose: So **"the works of God should be made manifest in him" (in you).**[5]

You've been wondering why for years? Maybe you haven't verbalized your bewilderment. But within your heart of hearts you've always speculated, hypothesized, and tried to give explanation to the "whys" of your reproductive history. And now, you have your answer. Just as God chose the unnamed blind man of John Chapter 9 to be His instrument of manifesting (making apparent and declaring) His great works, He, my friend, has graciously given to *you* that same task. *You* are His instrument, created by a Sovereign Craftsman who never makes a mistake, to seize every occurrence in your life as an opportunity to make His glory known to everyone. He has lovingly arranged every detail of every moment of your life with that purpose in mind. He wants you (and me) to glorify Him. His plan for us (and our infertility) is for the world to see the greatness of Himself through us. How awesome! He chose me! He chose you! He picked us! I've gone through 12 years of just about all the monster of infertility can think to offer me, and who knows what all you've experienced in your never ending duel with unsuccessful procreation – all with a Divine purpose in place.

> You are His instrument, created by a Sovereign Craftsman who never makes a mistake, to seize every occurrence in your life as an opportunity to make His glory known to everyone.

Our infertility has brought to us the calling, responsibility, and honor of glorifying the God of the Universe. Our just and proper perspective involves us no longer seeing ourselves as "victims" of our barrenness, but instead claiming for ourselves the status of being chosen by God for a Divine mission. Before time began, the God, who loves you with an inconceivable love, "ordered your steps" and handpicked you for this task.[6] You are promised throughout Scripture, that your days –and even your very steps – are guided, ordained, and directed by God (See Psalms 48:14, 139:16; Proverbs 16:9; 20:24.). And now, you get to let the Lord of All Lords make His wonderfulness known to those around you – via your infertility.

There are some 6.3 million women battling fertility issues.[7] That seems to be a lot, but when you consider the percentage in light of the number of child-bearing women, the figure is really small. We're certainly in the minority. Just a select few "made the cut," so to speak. There were only a few openings on this spiritual team, and we get to suit up for the big game. Oh how I pray my fastbreak of barrenness ends with a slamdunk for the cause of Christ!

Carefully and prayerfully consider these words penned by Saint Peter: **"In this you greatly rejoice, even though now for a little while, if necessary, you have been distressed by various trials, so that the proof of your faith, being more precious than gold which is perishable, even though tested by fire, may be found to result in praise and glory and honor at the revelation of Jesus Christ" (I Peter 1:6-7).**[8]

God used this passage in a marvelous way to strengthen my crippled soul. I was at one of my lowest points when the Lord seemed to inscribe upon my heart the truths found within these two simple verses. They are simple, yet so very profound and life changing. At the time, both of my sisters-in-law were pregnant. The entire dynamics of my family (on both sides) were changing completely. I was still grieving our third loss, another baby boy. It seemed my biological clock was ticking at a record pace, and I had never been so desperately alone in my life when the Lord spoke these words to me. I had read these Scriptures several times before, but when I read this passage while in my infertility pit, it was as if the Lord grabbed up my shuddering spirit, caressed it within His arms and soothingly rocked me into an unexplainable peace.

Here's how I read these words:

"In this you greatly rejoice" – I am to be rejoicing in this. What is my *this*? Well, you know ... this place of loneliness, isolation, grief, awkwardness, almost betrayal. God says I'm to be rejoicing here. Maybe not bouncing around with superficial laughter and glee, but I'm to be rejoicing – a sense of acceptance, maybe agreement, inner contentment and perhaps even expectancy. Rejoicing in the complexity of my infertility.

"Even though now for a little while" – Ah ha! This is only for a little while. It cannot and will not feel like this forever. It's a little while. Perhaps this craziness is almost over. (Now that's something I can rejoice in!)

"If necessary" – Oh, so this is all divinely *necessary*. God thinks all of this is *necessary*. All this pain – the endless nights spent crying alone on the couch, the countless vials of blood drawn testing hCG levels, the galore of baby showers that I *must* attend, the continual conversation of pregnancy happenings at family gatherings (in which I assume the role of a fifth wheel) – all this is needed? It must be!

"You (that's me) **have been distressed by various trials"** – Well, I'd say so! Distressed? Well, yeah! Various trials? Various? You know, and I know there is no end to the complexity of the matter at hand. Yet, God Almighty says I am to be rejoicing. This distressing trial is something about which to be rejoicing. It will only last a little while, and there is a plan in place! Now I'm feeling much better.

"So that the proof of your faith" – The plan here: my faith is being proven. Maybe proven to me. Maybe proven to the Lord. Maybe proven to others. I have a faith in the Lord, and as I encounter this storm, my faith is being proven.

"Being more precious than gold which is perishable, even though tested by fire" – This ordeal (or seeming nightmare, may be more fitting), this condition, this walk of life which is testing my faith, *God says*, is more precious than gold. Few things hold their value and beauty like gold. Yet it is noted here that gold, in comparison to my proven faith, is perishable. So there is a promise here from the Almighty Goldsmith of our hearts. The refining of our faith – by way of infertility and pregnancy loss – is beyond value and time constraints. Our proven faith that emerges from the inferno of loss and disappointment will never fade in its beauty and worth. There is a priceless and glorious outcome as we are in the fire and on the anvil belonging to God Almighty – a proven, precious, nonperishable faith. Now that is a hopeful thought!

Our proven faith that emerges from the inferno of loss and disappointment will never fade in its beauty and worth.

"May be found to result in praise and glory and honor at the revelation of Jesus Christ" – Ok, so now, more specifically, what is this promised by-product of our time spent at the Spiritual Goldsmith's? What exactly is God's intent of design for your various trials, better known as reproductive disappointments? Let's first see what it is not. Notice that the end result doesn't account for "a life that worked out as you had always hoped." The outcome doesn't refer to "a season of heartache followed by jubilant, new life." Nor is the result described as "God finally answering my prayer." No. No. God is intently and diligently at work within you and me. He is using His furnace of love and His tool of choice (in this case, our infertility) to chisel, reheat, mold, reheat, hammer, reheat, examine, reheat, and then perfect us into a masterpiece of His **praise, glory and honor**. Yes, my friend. May it be at the revelation of Jesus Christ, in the Presence of God Almighty, that our lives of infertility exhibit His matchless praise, glory and honor. There is great reason to rejoice in *this*!

> May it be at the revelation of Jesus Christ, in the Presence of God Almighty, that our lives of infertility exhibit His matchless praise, glory and honor.

The deliberation of the world around us is taking place. The majesty and beauty of Our Heavenly Father is in the running...and if it is my (or your) walk through infertility, as unsteady and sluggish as it may seem, that gets Him the deciding vote of praise, glory and honor – Oh, what a reason to rejoice!

I'm not sure exactly how the Lord plans for each woman to glorify Him with her infertile conditions and occurrences. I believe each case is unique, but over the years I have witnessed God's greatness becoming radiant through the lives of women struggling with infertility and pregnancy loss. He does have a plan, a plan to glorify Himself, and our prayer as His daughters should be one of surrender. Why don't you just surrender to His plan this very moment? I had to. I have to daily. After my third miscarriage, I had to come before the Lord (and I say *I had to* because my very life at that time stood in the balance) and yield to

His plan. My heart's dialogue with the God who loves me with no limits went a bit like this: *Lord, I get it. This all is from You – all the pain, all the loss, all the heartbreak. It is what You have chosen for me. You birthed me into this world, and You continue to sustain my every heartbeat and breath all for one purpose –to make Yourself look big, glorious, and wonderful. That is why I'm here, and You have fashioned every detail of my life to accomplish that one purpose. Lord, I want to fulfill Your purpose for me. God, if these three miscarriages are the way You want to glorify Yourself, then count me in. My heart is ever so willing, but I also know my flesh is weak. Make me strong, Jesus, and do Your work in me.*

This prayer may be a long way off for you. Believe me, I went through years of processing the pain before my heart could succumb to a surrender. Trust me, I wallowed in the pit of bitterness, loneliness, and anger for years. But for some reason (and I'm trusting this for you), when I finally understood the Lord's involvement in my infertility and a part of His Divine purpose, I was able to begin my healing. And now, my sweet sister, I'm praying with all earnestness that such a spiritual insight will begin to restore you. Your Heavenly Father handpicked you to glorify Him through your journey of infertility. Cling to that truth, friend. Begin now to consider recklessly and selflessly yielding to His plan. After all, only *you* are eligible and able for the mission. . . and *you* cannot afford to forfeit your benefits package by going spiritually AWOL!

About 12 years into my bout with infertility, I began to understand my Maker's twofold purpose for choosing the reproductive thorn for me. When my heart grasped the principle that my barrenness was brought to me **for God's glory**, I started on my road to recovery. My pregnancy disappointments were to project His greatness, and when I began to choose to live within this truth, it was as if my critically injured soul received its first treatment of a long awaited miracle drug. And praise the Lord, the second dose had been ordered and was on its way...

Principle One: Life is from God (and barrenness is too).

Principle Two: The Lord brought infertility into your life for His glory.

Chapter V

Principle Three: The Lord Brought Infertility into my Life . . . *For My Good*

Have I lost my mind? How can any of this be for my good? What good am I ever going to experience as a result of going through these years of loss, disappointment and heartache?

Reproductive problems can be so very cruel, as can be all disease – cancer, diabetes, multiple sclerosis, Alzheimer's – the list goes on. Truly, one of my most anticipated aspects of reigning with the Lord in His soon-coming Kingdom is the absence of health-related issues. I am so ready for the Lord of Lords to annihilate once and for all the Prince of this World, his demonic forces, and all the curses that are associated with living upon this fallen planet. I'm sick of hearing about people being diagnosed with cancer, reading on prayer lists about folks awaiting test results, and getting calls from girlfriends making sure I knew some little gal at our church was having a miscarriage. Physical sickness and disease are not fun – at all!

If you have encountered any amount of pregnancy complications, you have come to know first-hand just how brutal reproductive illness can be. Infertility and pregnancy loss have the potential to sling their victim to the ground, pound her relentlessly with their fists, take a few steps in retreat, and then return to kick their bloody prey into an emotional coma. We all have our war stories – accounts of just how wicked infertility can be. Many times, I have lain on exam tables with my feet in those horrible stirrups, while watching images on a monitor and thinking to myself, *Dear God, how much worse can this get?* I've literally crawled into the backseat of my parents' SUV bound for the emergency room, writhing from excruciating abdominal pain as uterine contractions violently forced a catheter (that my doctor insisted I leave inserted until my next visit) into my cervix that wasn't dilating. I've stood at the register of a department store awaiting a refund for the armful of brand-new maternity clothes that I would no longer be needing. I've had my glorious hopes of a healthy pregnancy confidently confirmed by a world-renowned fetal medicine specialist, only to have those same hopes destroyed by *another* unexplainable miscarriage just 60 hours later. I've watched my husband mail payment after payment to doctors and hospitals to pay for medical services for the baby we never got to bring home from the hospital. From time to time, it all seems a bit ruthless and unmerciful to me. I've felt every vicious blow of my infertility, and I'm sure you've felt yours, too. Many of your experiences are surely different from mine, but it is certain you have been wounded by the cruelty of reproductive issues.

So, how can it all be **for my good? For your good?** If we allow our carnal minds to process our most traumatic moments in the valley of infertility, we will never be able to recognize "our good." However, if we pursue "Part B" of our two-fold explanation with just a dab of Biblical thinking, we will be able to identify "our good" through our reproductive calamity.

What is the world's most-loved Bible verse? Surely, all ages claim **John 3:16: "For God so loved the world, that He gave His only begotten Son, that whosoever believeth in Him, should not perish but have everlasting life."** Many people, some who know the Lord and some who don't, can quote this life-giving verse. But when you survey "more spiritual circles," perhaps a ladies' Bible study group, an online chatroom comprised of women of the faith or even Christian bookstore patrons, you discover another most-loved passage. Can you quote it? **Romans 8:28: "And we know that all things work together for good to them that love God, to them who are called according to His purpose."** Truly this is one of my favorite verses. I've lived under its promise all of my life. I can still visualize the oversized antique library table in the living room of my childhood home. There, sitting on a crocheted doily, in a stately fashion was the table's focal piece – a delicate, yet dignified print of the beloved passage, embellished with ornate lettering and perfectly framed in a wooden oval. Its words were engrafted within my heart from an early age. I believed then, and I believe now, without a doubt that all things *do* work for the good of those who love God and are called according to His purpose.

I've thought about this verse often over the years. As "tragedy" came in various degrees (from our pet dog getting run over to me not being in the homecoming court), I would reflect upon this verse. I wanted its blessing, its hope, its promise. I wanted to fall within the criteria of those receiving the good. I'd often evaluate myself making sure I *did* love God and that I *was* called according to His purpose.

"Love God." It seems it has always been easy for me to love the Lord. Thankfully, I grew up in a home that introduced me early to the sacrifice of Jesus, and throughout my life (even early childhood), I've always had within my heart a sincere love for the man who went through so much for me at Calvary. But when it comes to "being called according to His purpose," that's been a condition with which I've struggled. The phrase means to adapt one's lifestyle to "fit into" the plans of God, to surrender to a Godly perspective or mind-set and to fashion the intent of one's lifestyle accordingly.[1] As I would (and still do) critique my faithfulness to the Lord, I admit then (and still do) that I, regretfully and shamefully, fail in many areas. Many times, I do not choose His purposes for my daily walk. However, I am confident that I have been graciously called, and I have redirected my life as a whole according to His purposes. So with all praise and glory going to my Sweet Lord, I've personally been able to claim the promise of this dearly loved verse for many years.

But it wasn't until the tenth year of my encounter with infertility that I began to question the surety of the "Roman 8:28 principle." Yes, I still loved God, and I was still living with a calling to His purposes. I was teaching Sunday School, reading my Bible, praying, being a good wife (cleaning, cooking, doing laundry), going to Bible Studies, etc. I had not changed; I still passed the spiritual checklist of the Romans 8:28 recipients. But in no way, shape, form or fashion was I able to recognize my reproductive issues as "good" for me. To me, none of it was good; it certainly was not "for my good." I couldn't see *any* good in *any* of it, for *any*one – as far as that mattered. The procedures, tests, surgeries, bed rest, complications and ultimately the loss of the babies I had grown to love with an indescribable love - *all* of it was horrific and more painful than imaginable. The print on our library table had become a simple decorating accessory; my infertility had left me spiritually blinded, and I could see no validity in the "good" of Romans 8:28.

You may be there, sweet sister. This may be the condition of your heart at this very moment. You might be at your very end. Perhaps, your infertility has left you drowning in a sea of unbelief, and now you're turning your back to any spiritual life-saving rings that you've grabbed onto over the years. The assurances in God's Word may seem a bit unstable (maybe even complicated) to you. But, please, dear one, let me encourage you to stop your toiling. Cease your striving. End your resisting. And allow your Heavenly Father to rescue your very soul. He has a plan for you, and wrestling in the rip current of doubt is not in that plan. Commit to your rescue. Lunge toward your heart's life-boat and let the Lover of your Soul tow you back to safety. The fierce waves of infertility have been known to take many lives over the years. But a life-line of survival has been issued. It is right before you. Grab ahold and hang on for all your worth.

All aspects of your journey with infertility, all you have endured, all you may currently be enduring, and all you will endure is for your good.

It IS true! All of your pregnancy-related trials ARE **for your good**. There is no need to recant your faith, burn your Bible or post your thesis of disbelief on your church's doors. Roman 8:28 is so very true. All things *do* work for your good. (Note: I'm assuming that you are complying to the requirements for the promise's beneficiaries – loving God and being called according to His purpose.) All aspects of your journey with infertility, all you have endured, all you may currently be enduring, and all you will endure *is* **for your good**.

Now, won't you spiritually plunge with me into the foundation of this promise? After all, the truth of this one passage may be the extended hand that potentially pulls you to your soul's place of rest and safety. Read it again. **"And we know that all things work together for good to them that love God, to them who are called according to His purpose."** Romans 8:28

When you study the verb tense of this verse, you will discover a perfect, imperative condition, meaning that the applied action is continual and deliberate in nature. We read here of a God who began and continues indefinitely with the action. Some manuscripts emphasize the Greek word (sunergeo)[2], from which *work* is derived, and read "God is continually working in all things for the good..." This consideration indicates a sense of God working with, cooperating with all things for good. So, we must apply the issue at hand to this truth. God has begun, and He is continually at work within all aspects of your life – specifically, your reproductive challenges. Whatever they have been in the past and whatever they may currently be, God is constantly working in and through them. The passage clearly states, God is working in all things. And as my dear mentor, who is also the assistant of Precept Ministries' founder, Kay Arthur, explains in her lectures given around the world – "the Greek word for *all* is *all!*" So, the *all* here encompasses every detail of your pregnancy-related issues. Every loss, every doctor's appointment, every unattended baby shower, and even your every emotion are all being *worked with* by a Sovereign God for your good.

Is that convincing? Are you seeing the hope of a gracious God, who loves you enough to sacrifice His only Son, deliberately starting and continuing to work all aspects of your infertility for your good? It is redeeming; isn't it, my friend? The same God, who provided the "indescribable gift" of Calvary, the same God who stirred your heart to a saving faith and the same God who has walked everyday beside you since your re-birth in Him, is at work now and forever within you, taking *every* facet of *every* phase of your infertility and destining it for *your good*. (II Corinthians 9:15)[3] Are you liking the sound of that? I sure do.

We understand now that God is at work through our reproductive hardships. I'm thinking that I must have really kept Him busy during the past twelve years! But isn't He so amazing? Just think. At the exact moment I was undergoing a uterine biopsy via a water ultrasound (and thought I'd literally die from the pain), "Tara" might have been at her family reunion trying to rejoice in her promiscuous 16-year-old niece's pregnancy, "Jessica" could have been awaiting a crucial phone call from the geneticist, "Mandy" might have been staring at another single line on a pregnancy test, and who knows where that one moment found *you*. But in it all, as complex as each of our simultaneous infertility happenings might have been, God was right there, on task, working in it all for our good.

Now for the real "kicker" of the Romans 8:28 insight. The *good*. What exactly is the definition of *good* in this text? As I've clung to this passage over the years, I've often wanted to define the *good* as a specified positive result in my life. I'm sure you've done this too. A *difficult* situation entered your life; you claimed the outcome of Romans 8:28 and speculated a specific *good* result. Our human minds want the *good* promised for us, but we tend to allow our personal preferences of that *good* to become the hope to which we cling. Unintentionally, in our times of distress, we take the prescribed *good* and tweak it to our liking. (Doesn't that sound better than *manipulate* it?) We anxiously anticipate a *good* situation or scenario, yet we often formulate within our minds an outcome that seems suitable to us.

Aren't we all too often guilty of doing this as we face reproductive disappointments? How many times have you and I been able to finally stop crying and fall asleep when we've begun to assure ourselves that our speculated *good* is just around the corner? I've heard the hopeful affirmations within my mind time and time again. "It's all ok. Next month will be perfect. Then, the baby will be born around Mother's Day." "It's just implantation bleeding. She's just making her nest. Very common. No worries. We'll get that perfect ultrasound in a few weeks." "Thirty-six now? Go back to sleep. Rhonda had Kyle when she was 41. There's still plenty of time. It's gonna work!" You see how we do this? It's undeniable; isn't it? Our finite, earthly intellect has pre-programmed us to this tendency. But, as daughters of the Heavenly Father, our crisis of belief usually follows the realization that **our** expected *good* is not going to be actualized in the story line of our infertility.

I did not have a baby around Mother's Day. The early spotting may have just been implantation bleeding, but I lost the baby anyway (even after the "normal" ultrasound). And there's no chance I'll successfully carry and deliver a child by my 42nd birthday. My *goods* did not come to fruition. And, sweet friend, I'm sure you're sitting there nodding your head; many of your envisioned *good* outcomes never came to be either. Have we, as the Christian community, misinterpreted this promise? Have we taken Romans 8:28 out of context? Is there some mystery to its truth that we have left uncovered? Why have we witnessed our *goods* not being actualized?

Are you ready for the answer? Allow God's Holy Word to unlock a truth that will lead you to fall wildly in love with this verse that you've always cherished. Yes, all things do work together for good to those who love the Lord and are called according to His purpose. It is a guarantee!

Always! But the *good* is not limited to what your mind and my mind devises. Thank the Lord! Instead, the God of the Universe, whose thoughts and ways transcend all human comprehension, gets to determine the *good*. The Promise Provider gets to define *good*. And isn't that so okay with you? I'm delighted in this idea. Why on earth would I (in my limited, carnal state) want to stipulate any facet of my life's destiny in exchange for the supernatural, infinite arrangements being availed to me by an All-Knowing, All-Powerful, All-Loving God? **His** *good* is the *good* I want!

So, what is *His* good? Its simple, yet incredibly insightful, definition is beautifully defined in the next verse, Verse 29, **"For those whom He foreknew, He also predestined to become conformed to the image of His Son, so that He would be the firstborn among many brethren."**[4]*Good* is defined here. The *good* of verse 28 means *becoming conformed to the image of His Son. Good* is you and I, God's children, becoming more and more like Jesus. Christ-likeness is not just a positive, good outcome for the events and situations of our lives, but it is truly the very best thing that can happen to any of us! Our brilliant Manufacturer has a finished creation in mind; that completed project is perfect, flawless and unequivocally marvelous in design. The finalized product, if you will, is a state of you and me being ridded of our fleshly tendencies and you and I functioning in total surrender to the mind and will of Christ. That is our Maker's "dream creation," His ultimate intent of design. The promised *good* that results from every event and circumstance of our lives is that we become more and more like Jesus Christ. God Almighty is diligently and continuously at work, shaping us into His Christ-like creation. He is orchestrating and utilizing every facet of our lives to mold us into a likeness of Jesus Christ. And our conforming to that image *is* what is best for us. If portraying the nature of Christ is the prominent, Divine objective of our total existence, wouldn't you agree that the *good* of Romans 8:28 (as defined by God) far exceeds the worth of our petty, finite expectations?

Consider this scenario: My MaMaw has to have surgery. The surgery being successful is what my human heart perceives as *good* for me. That is *my* desired outcome formulated by my feeble, limited, and fleshly capacity with only a fraction of knowledge and insight into the present. A successful surgery for MaMaw is *my* definition of *good*. And in light of the vast knowledge of God and his ability to foreknow the big picture of our lives, surely we'd opt to receive *His* definition of *good*. The *good*, that ultimately becomes the *best* by far, is our Creator thoughtfully chiseling away our sinfulness and then gently sculpting into us a characteristic of His perfect Son. How easy it is for our awareness of God's understanding of *good* to become tainted by our mortal thinking.

> God Almighty is diligently and continuously at work, shaping us into His Christ-like creation. He is orchestrating and utilizing every facet of our lives to mold us into a likeness of Jesus Christ.

So, MaMaw *did* make it through the surgery. How do we explain it if *our* interpretation of *good* is the actual outcome? That is simple, my friend. Sometimes **our good** (perhaps MaMaw's recovery) coincides and "fits within" **God's** *good* (me becoming more like Christ). Many times we are able to see our preferences for *good* become reality because those particular circumstances accomplish His definition of *good*. For example, MaMaw made a full recovery, and God used that specific outcome to make me more like Christ. Or it may not have been this specific, but perhaps ... MaMaw's healing might have become a personal experience that I would later use to share the gospel. Her healing could have possibly become a stepping stone for my spiritual development, making me a better verbal witness. Do you see how this works? We *do* get to live, many times, within our situations of *good* when those particular outcomes lead us into a likeness of Christ. What we anticipate as a *good* ending ultimately becomes a part of the *best* ending – which is you and I conforming to Jesus' image.

However, there are times when God's master design of us reflecting Christ does not include the fulfillment of our humanly-desired outcome. Your infertility may have proven this to you. God's big picture of us becoming like Christ is the trump; you and I resembling *self* less and *Christ* more catches all other tricks. If MaMaw's recuperation (as much as I wanted it) wasn't a part of God's plan to make me more like Jesus, then her getting better wouldn't have been a potential conclusion.

Oh how I pray this is making sense. Your situation may look like this: All of your hopes for your second pregnancy may have become reality, and now you're loving every minute of raising your baby in the nurture and admonition of the Lord. You reflect upon your life as a parent, and you can easily, yet humbly, see how you resemble Christ more now than years ago. Now, as that sweet child naps, you've found yourself committed to a daily time spent in God's Word. Your heart's desire of getting your baby was met, and you are growing in Christ and progressing in your conformity to His image.

But your third and fourth pregnancies may have slightly different outcomes. Your latter efforts of procreation may have both ended in medically-unexplainable miscarriages. Your idea of *good* certainly wasn't the end result, *but* you know now, without a doubt, that God used your losses to shape you into the image of Jesus. It may not be in a huge, radical transformation that has placed you on the platform at religious stadium events, but since your agonizing pregnancy defeats, you've been faithful to extend sympathy to other hurting families as they've encountered miscarriage. Now, you are ministering in Christ-likeness through cards and visits, truly fulfilling the plan of **II Corinthians 1:3-4: "Blessed be the God and Father of our Lord Jesus Christ, the Father of mercies and God of all comfort, who comforts us in all our affliction so that we will be able to comfort those who are in any affliction with the comfort with which we ourselves are comforted by God."**[5]

Do you see His plan? He wants you and me to be like Jesus – look like Jesus, love like Jesus, live like Jesus. That is the *good* our Abba Father is so diligently striving to bring to us by endlessly working through all the occurrences of our lives. Whatever is written upon the pages of your infertility story – regardless of how insignificant or monumental each event may seem to have been – the guaranteed outcome is **for your good**. And that *good* is a conformity to the image of Christ. May we surrender to the heavenly process. **"And I am sure of this, that He who began a good work in you will bring it to completion at the day of Jesus Christ." (Philippians 1:6)**[6]

One day, when we stand before the Lord, the spinning of the Potter's wheel will cease, and the clay-covered, nail-scarred hands of our Savior will be washed – once and for all. The Master's work will be complete, and all of His

redeemed will finally exist as intended. For truly, we will
see Him as He is! (I John 3:2) As for now, friend, please
know that no matter where you are in your infertility
journey, the work is in progress! And if you listen carefully, you can hear the rhythmic cadence of His spinning
wheel. You hear it? Sounds like it's getting slower. And
slower. And slower. His masterpiece is almost finished.

Principle One: Life is from God (and barrenness is too).

Principle Two: The Lord brought infertility into your life for His glory.

Principle Three: The Lord brought infertility into your life for your good.

The Chain is Being Broken

Infertility can become a restrictive bondage for anyone
and has the potential of ultimately rendering one para-
lyzed. In my situation, the years of loss had left me somewhat imprisoned. The complicated reproductive events of
more than a decade of my life had become a heavy, bigger-
than-life chain that seemed to start at my feet and twist
up my body making me completely immovable. But as the
Lord began to reveal to me Biblical principles that I had
never encountered, it was as if the enormous, seemingly-
permanent shackle began to be destroyed one link at a
time. When I understood that life *and barrenness* were
from God, the top, end links that restrained my head,
neck, and shoulders were severed. As I meditated upon
the truth of my barrenness being for God's glory, the next,
weighty links that restricted my stiff arms and entrapped

But as the Lord began to reveal to me Biblical principles that I had never encountered, it was as if the enormous, seemingly-permanent shackle began to be destroyed one link at a time. torso were ripped at their wielded seams. When I realized my infertility was an instrument to bring about my *good*, and when I grasped the true definition of *good*, I was freed from the bottom links that had been wrapped tightly around my legs and feet for so many years. My freedom began, and I welcomed my newly-found liberation. And oh, how I earnestly pray for you, too, my sister ... that as the same truths have been presented to you, you will allow your tender heart to wholly accept each reality and then watch as your chain of bondage falls powerlessly to your feet, leaving you free.

Chapter VI
Keep That Door Shut!

I'm sure within your history of infertility and/or pregnancy loss, there have been certain happenings that you want to never think about again. There are those extreme moments of terror and hurt that you strive never to re-visit mentally. These events or circumstances become like a violent intruder that we desperately try to keep shoved behind a closed door. With intense fervor, we lean upon the door with all of our weight; our extended foot is scotched at its base; our shoulders are relentlessly pressed on its panels, and both of our fists are clinched around its knob that we are determined to keep unturned. The event or situation was absolutely horrific; it either terrified us or devastated our hopeful spirits. And although we may have successfully worked through our past, we still daily resist with all effort that one *episode* (whatever it may be) from our consciousness. We continue to live and progress through other land-marks of our lives, but that sole painful or scary affair is kept behind the closed doors of our minds. We strive to continue on with our lives while attempting to not even recognize – much less recall – that distressing incident.

Simply stated: The said occurrence was so excruciating that we hope to dismiss its very existence completely from our life's story.

Does your story of infertility contain one of these traumatic situations? Perhaps it was a visit to a heartless hematologist who in the process of testing for a clotting disorder led you to believe another underlying disease, maybe even leukemia, could be present. Maybe the moment you've locked behind closed doors consists of your split-second glance into the face of the ultrasound gal whose eyes quickly revealed to you the loss of your precious baby. Or it could be that your dismissed tragedy is a midnight arrival to the ER and everything associated with that night when you had your second miscarriage. Your reproductive past may include months of pregnancy-related catastrophes, and those big chunks of time have had to be removed purposely from your consciousness. I'm sure you can relate. There are times that the pain and fear are so horrendous, that in order for us to cope, we *must* attempt to isolate those moments in time and forever discard them from our memories. In order for our physical and emotional health to be maintained, we, the survivors of infertility, *must* keep those doors shut.

The unwritten chronicles of your life and my life could look like this. There is a long corridor of experiences, from birth to the present. Lining the corridor are thresholds that lead to a variety of events (both good and bad) – our first lost tooth, the tornado of '96, our sweet sixteen birthday, the death of a cherished loved one, our salvation experience, our wedding, etc. As we mentally stroll down our life's hallway, we gaze into the rooms from the past and relive the glorious moments. But as we approach the opened doorway exposing the gloomy times, we can *thankfully* just peek in long enough to recognize God's mercy and then walk hastily on to the next entrance. However, along the way, there is that closed door. And regardless of how long ago we encountered the cruel intruder now locked behind the door, we still *must* keep that door shut!

I dread cracking open my closed door. So far in this book, I've only referenced three-fourths of my pregnancy disappointments. However, my history of infertility has a soul-shaking experience behind a shut, locked door. I'm able to reenter the rooms containing my first three losses, but I hesitate to approach mentally the locked door leading to my fourth and final miscarriage – the one that left me barren forever.

A Family Christmas Trip –
Too Much Fun!

A few years ago, my family decided to forgo the "gift-giving" aspect of Christmas. We all got tired of having to dredge through crowded shopping malls, in search of gifts for people who didn't need a thing. We vowed to stop giving gifts and start spending more time together as a family. Instead of spending money on needless presents, our parents would "treat" us all to a few days of vacation. Sounds like a great deal; doesn't it?

So a couple of weeks before Christmas 2009, we all loaded up – me and Rusty, Mom and Dad, Jon Paul and Erin, my two too-much-fun nephews, and you guessed it – our little Granny! We headed to a quaint, lakeside resort in Kentucky for a few days of much-needed rest and family time.

At this time, I was thirty-eight, and it had been six years since my last (third) miscarriage. With my third miscarriage, I had seen a high-risk specialist in Nashville. After the pregnancy was deemed non-viable he performed a D & C, and during the surgery, he "felt" some uterine tissue that seemed abnormal. (I still don't understand those "blind" procedures. Doesn't it seem like a surgeon should be able to *see* what he is working on?) A few weeks later, he did a water hysterosonogram and discovered a small spot in the upper corner of my uterus that contained some unidentifiable tissue.

Now, let me back up with a detail or two. From the "get go," this doctor was very pessimistic. Upon every visit, I would leave with suspicion of some scary, new "factor" that he was "trying to rule out." He tested and tested and referred and referred until he almost drove me crazy! I genuinely praise the Lord that all tests came back normal, but the process of wading through all of the pessimism left me (and Rusty) very, very hesitant about ever wanting to pursue another pregnancy – which this doctor predicted would ultimately not work out.

Although he never was able to identify this spot in my uterus, he did advise me concerning a future pregnancy. I'll never forget the conversation (or better yet, his monologue) in which he informed me I was a candidate for a cornual pregnancy. He warned of a future pregnancy that could cause a type of rupture within my uterus and/or fallopian tube. He stated if I ever did get pregnant again, I would need to stay close to Nashville during the first eight weeks of my pregnancy ...Why? Are you ready for this? ... Just in case I started to bleed to death. Yes, that is what I was told by the doctor who I soon QUIT seeing!

I then went back to my trusted endocrinologist who had actually *looked* in my uterus during a previous myomectomy. He tried to assure me the mysterious spot was only scar tissue. But I still had heard the prediction. From a specialist. I had been made aware of a scary possibility, and my mind began to forecast the bad scenario. Pregnancy and death. In a round about way, these two possibilities were connected for me.

After our third loss, Rusty and I put the "family" idea on the back burner. To be honest, my third miscarriage and my visits to the "World's Scariest OB-GYN" left us both very skeptical. We never really discussed the life-threatening "what if's" my doctor described, but Rusty knew I didn't want to bleed to death. The scenarios that were mentioned in the doctor's office were so horrifying, Rusty and I didn't even want to verbalize them. We still had a rich, blessed life (even without children), and although it went unsaid, we didn't want to risk losing what we had – even life itself – with another pregnancy. The track record on past pregnancies had not been good. And if history is an indicator of the future, we couldn't justify taking the risk.

So that is where we were in our procreative mindset at the time. I still desperately wanted to be a mom. I still missed my babies. I still didn't want to go through life as a childless wife. I still had sleepless nights filled with grief and concern, but I literally had the *life* – at least the willingness to be remotely a part of forming one – scared out of me. For the next four years, Rusty and I took great efforts *not* to get pregnant. We had not considered and certainly had not desired any finality related to our child-lessness, but we still were not to the place where we could move forward with new life possibilities.

So, here's the Moody clan. Staying in Cabin #518. En-joying the Christmas lights, pancake breakfasts and my nephew's original puppet shows. As a family, we were basking in God's goodness, treasuring the "good times" with each other and especially the presence of sweet Granny, who was about to turn 85. You know where this is headed; don't you?

I'm late! I'm never late! I'm a *day* late! Rusty was totally nonchalant. He didn't even remotely acknowledge a possibility of me being pregnant. Although Rusty said the purchase was completely ridiculous, I did manage to get him to sneak off to the pharmacy with me to get "nose spray." Really – we *did* buy some nose spray, but we also arrived back at the cabin with a pregnancy test. Casually, we entered the kitchen, greeted our family, proceeded straight to our room, shut the door, and I headed for the toilet. Still all the while, the thought of me being pregnant had not come within a sixty-mile radius of Rusty's head. He was O-U-T, and that spells *out*.

> I'm late!
> I'm never late!
> I'm a day late!

You know how this works: I peed on the stick, and the waiting process began. I couldn't bear to look at the indicator windows alone, so I quickly laid the test on the countertop and covered it up with a white hand towel. I left the bathroom, and told Rusty we were going to go back in there *together* and see the results. (After all, if I *was* pregnant we *both* had gotten ourselves in the mess. That was my thinking.) Rusty rolled his eyes, shook his head and gave me his "OK, whatever you say" agreement. In his mind, our trip to buy a pregnancy test (and then actually take the test) was my over-reacting, being ridiculous and wasting twenty bucks; yet he complied to enter the bathroom for the Grand Reveal.

I'll never forget as long as I live the moments that followed me jerking the towel off that test. There I saw an image that brought sheer terror to my marriage ... double lines! I was pregnant. Every emotion from confusion, to fear, to bewilderment, to horror struck us so powerfully that we both were speechless and immobile. I somehow made it to the bed, sat down, covered my face in my hands, shook my head, and repeatedly said, "I can't believe it. I'm pregnant." Rusty was so quiet. He turned from the bathroom, and for the first time in eighteen years, I sensed a genuine fear taking over my strong, "I can fix it" husband. Now, my Rusty Farmer is a man's man. Big. Burly. And if I can say so myself, this man I married, by whom I still am completely smitten, is one of the toughest guys I know. He's strong, and I can only recall one occasion that I've ever seen him scared. For 12 years, we had been through many alarming and concerning events related to my infertility. And with each experience, I never once believed Rusty to be afraid. No matter the procedure or possible diagnosis, Rusty was always calm, reassuring, and truly at peace. Whenever I was taken with fear and unbelief, the Lord would use Rusty's sincere faith and optimism to bring me peace. During any crisis, especially those related to my infertility, Rusty would always persuade me to join him in "looking on the bright side." That's just the way we had worked as a couple over the years. The Lord ingeniously crafted Rusty for me – by giving him the much-needed composure and confidence I so frequently lacked. But in the master suite of Green Turtle Bay's Cabin # 518, I saw the weakness of my strapping man. Concern and total shock was overtaking him. This time Rusty wasn't seeing the "bright side" of life, and this new dynamic with my husband left me totally lost. Genuine fear had a death grip on Rusty, and that alone shook me to my very core.

Our lovely, paradise bedroom overlooking the tranquil Kentucky Lake became filled with disbelief and panic. But, thank the Lord for some spiritual "roots," as shallow as they may be, we both knew any solace would have to come from the Lord. I'm not sure of the exact time frame for all of these details, but at some point, Rusty and I lay together on the bed and mustered up enough sanity to hold each other and pray. We needed the Lord right then, and we surely were going to need Him as this pregnancy progressed.

"How on earth did I get pregnant?" I consider myself to be somewhat knowledgeable when it comes to biological life cycles. After all, I took quite a few upper level biology classes in college; I've taught science for years; I breezed through seventh grade sex education, and like anyone undergoing fertility treatment, I had become a student of the human reproductive process. But I still found myself asking, "How?"

Within moments of our unexpected EPT encounter, Rusty and I began to be introduced to a battery of circumstances that supernaturally assured us this pregnancy was entirely Divine. Yes, I know. All pregnancies are entirely Divine; God is completely responsible for every aspect of new life. But as you will see, and as we daily discovered, there were several exceptional details related to this particular pregnancy – details that by no means could be explained as coincidental. And as Rusty and I discovered these "God-incidents," our faith began to grow, and we became assured; no doubt about it – this was the one! I was going to have this baby!

Rusty and I knew we must tell my family. We were on a family trip, for heaven's sakes, and there was no way we were going to be able to cover-up the emotions created by the double-lined indicator window. I went to the door; I'm sure I was all red-eyed and frazzled-looking. I had all intentions of going into the "great room" of the cabin and announcing to everyone all at one time that I was pregnant. But I just couldn't do it. Upon opening the door, I saw my mom. As our eyes met, I began to shake my head, the tears started rolling, and I motioned for her to come. I stood there like a timid, little eight-year-old girl who had to tell her Mommy that she accidentally had broken great-grandma's antique plate. How silly! But upon my mother learning that I was pregnant, Rusty and I received our first non-coincidental assurance that we were "gonna" have this baby.

There were moments in our mother/daughter/son-in-law discussion that I don't want to recall; some were terribly faithless and ugly. But what I do want to remember is what my sweet momma said as tears came down her face ... "Oh, Candise, I think this is wonderful." And then she shared about an experience she had with the Lord a long time ago while she was walking her driveway. She said she had really become overly burdened with our child-lessness, and one day as she walked and talked with the Lord, He released her from that concern. In a confirmation to her spirit – not in an audible voice – God plainly assured her that He was going to take care of our "baby issue." Divine Incident #1 – God told Momma. This is it! We might as well get ready. We are having a baby!

As the days passed, we received and identified assurance after assurance that God had destined this baby into our lives. Some of these confirmations took place prior to me even knowing I was pregnant. Divine Incident #2 – About two weeks before we discovered I was pregnant (which as you know, would possibly be around the conception time), I taught a Life Group lesson that suggested using three introductory questions:

1) If you could go anywhere, where would you go?

2) If you could do anything, what would you do?

3) If you could have anything, what would you have?

As I prepared the lesson, I became convicted to answer these questions for myself. If I was going to challenge my girls to consider them, then I surely needed to, as well. So as I finished preparing the lesson, I thought of my answer. It was so easy. With no hesitation, I quickly and certainly identified my greatest desire in life would be to have a healthy baby with Rusty Farmer, my life's love. The greatest thing I could do or have did not include adopting another couple's baby; I wanted our own baby – and a healthy one. I taught this lesson with this realization in mind. I had no thoughts about this desire becoming actualized. I had only acknowledged the most prominent yearning of my life.

The timing and content of such a Life Group lesson may not be a substantial confirmation for many folks. But it was for me. When Rusty and I were in the "how did this happen" stage and trying to wrap our minds around my pregnancy, I would think back upon this timely lesson which caused me to admit my life's longing. Could it be? This lesson? These three questions? The timing? Not a coincident, but rather a God-incident verifying this was not *my* normal pregnancy.

There were several more occurrences that Rusty and I began to "hang our hats on." With the three previous losses, we were a bit preprogrammed to search for and cling to any form of assurance. Perhaps we "banked" too much on these circumstances. Perhaps we were so desperate for assurance that we mistook ordinary happenings as Providential confirmations. Whatever the case, we needed optimism. Here's a brief account of some events we interpreted as promising: (I believe you'll see their relevancy.)

When I was pregnant (yet unaware of it), my dear friend and sole "partner-in-infertility," Rebecca came to visit us. I watched for three days as she and her husband interacted with their miracle baby girl (who was then a senior in high school). It was simply beautiful and inspiring to behold ... a mother and father still jubilant over the life God had entrusted to them. I had no idea I was pregnant, but that weekend served as a comfort to me. How *coincidental*? No. It had to be *God-incidental*. Why else would this family who overcame infertility be sent to our home this particular weekend – the first weekend I'm actually pregnant? It's a God-thing!

How about this one? The Wednesday prior to our Green Turtle Bay trip and all that entailed, we had a special guest speaker in our mid-week student service at church. Our students had been studying the book of Job, and we were bringing in a modern-day account of dealing with tragedy via a precious lady. Sandy didn't marry until she was 36. She had their first child, Justin, at 38. Justin was born with Down's Syndrome, and after five tough years of medical complications, he got to go live in Heaven. Sandy recounted to the students her family's calamity, and God was certainly glorified. Sandy's testimony also included another *gift* she and Jim received – Kayla Renee. Yes, at forty-two, Sandy gave birth to a super-healthy baby from Heaven. Kayla grew into a lovely young woman of God. I listened to Sandy's testimony that evening, thinking then and then re-thinking again and again about the hope of being forty-two and having a *Kayla Clary*. God had to be confirming ... the nature of this testimony ... its timing. It was more than ironic; it was Divine. Was it all supernaturally orchestrated? I sat among high school students and listened to a procreative success story, all the while a new life (only of which God knew) developed inside of me.

And here's one more, but, oh, so promising a circumstance Rusty and I interpreted as a whisper from God verifying the reality of our family's new addition. About the time our baby was conceived, Rusty got a call from RV Brown. RV is an anointed evangelist that Rusty and I had gotten to know some fifteen years earlier. Over the years, Rusty and I had served with RV at youth camps, community-wide crusades, Fellowship of Christian Athletes events, and school assemblies. Some of Rusty's favorite times were fishing trips with RV – not to mention the home-cooked fish dinners they enjoyed after a day on the lake. RV and his family moved to Florida, and we hadn't heard from him in about six years. About the time our baby was conceived, Rusty got a call from his long-lost fishing buddy. They chatted a while, and RV ended up sending Rusty a copy of his new book. Keep in mind: Rusty is not an avid reader. I've only known him to read maybe two books – outside of the Bible – during our entire marriage. As soon as Rusty got RV's book, he devoured it. I'd see Rusty reading, and I would think: *Rusty is being a good friend. I guess the only reason he's reading it is because he doesn't want to hurt RV's feelings; the next time they talk, Rusty wants to be able to thank him for the book and let RV know how great he did writing it. Rusty really has no interest in its topic or any use for its content.* You want to know the title of the book? *Step Up to the Plate, Dad!* We knew the Lord knew what He was doing; He had Rusty reading his first parenting book as our tiny baby was being formed. It was just another Divine Incident that we eagerly interpreted as a promise for a pregnancy that would be unconventional – for me.

There were "lots" of little occurrences, such as these. Tiny details that could have possibly been coincidental or insignificant. But Rusty and I identified them as assurances from the Creator that a healthy baby was on the way.

It had been almost six years since Rusty and I had made a pregnancy announcement, and like us, our friends and family had mentally put that possibility on hold. So as we began to tell folks I was pregnant again, we got a lot of "wow" responses. Rusty and I were still trying to convince ourselves everything was going to work out, and as we shared with our loved ones and closest friends some of these God-incidents (Mom's driveway revelation, RV's book, Rebecca and Jim's visit, Sandy's timely testimony), we became more and more reassured that *this* time was going to be different; I was having this baby. And as our news began to spread, we encountered no one who was skeptical. Everyone had a good feeling about this one – even my OB nurse practitioner. Oh, and by the way, my Biblical counselors (the man and his wife who I believe are closer to God than anyone I know) sent a text on December 11 that read: *Congratulations!!!! We have been praying for this!!!!! We will continue to lift you up to His throne.* Bro. Joe and Mrs. Gail? They had been praying for this? Their prayers got answered!

Chapter VII

Here We Go Again

For several days, Rusty and I let our "Divine incidents" and the optimism of our loved ones and friends lift our hopes to record heights. The promise of *finally* a new life was soaring high above any doubts. But on Wednesday, December 16, we watched our faith-filled anticipation crash and burn. I woke up that morning to spotting. *Please, God, not again!*

In an instant, all hopeful expectancy was gone, and I began to prepare myself for the inevitable end. What else could I expect? I'm now four for four with this. I get pregnant. I go a week or two. Start spotting. And then it all goes downhill from there. My fourth pregnancy quickly became somewhat familiar (but certainly not routine) to us ... I was spotting again. Rusty and I get in the truck and head to the clinic (about 25 miles away). That's how this works.

Our transit to the doctor's office was surreal for us; although we had faced this same scenario multiple times before, it all seemed a bit foreign that day. I lay down in the back seat while Rusty drove. I can remember looking up at him and hearing him say, "This just doesn't make sense – why God would do all of this." I could see the frustration and concern on his face.

Even if you are a newcomer to the struggles of infertility, you are completely aware of the ups and downs related to this issue. Rusty and I had enjoyed the few days of total trust in the certainty of our family's upcoming addition. And now we were victims of utter despair and hopelessness. Infertility truly is the ride of a lifetime. Each day has the potential to bring a never-ending cycle of ups and downs, ups and downs. Circumstances can change drastically from day to day, and with that, the emotional status of a hopeful mother-to-be can violently swing from the highest of highs to the lowest of lows. You know how it all operates; the happiest moment of your life can suddenly be followed by the darkest moment of your life, and vice versa.

> Even if you are a newcomer to the struggles of infertility, you are completely aware of the ups and downs related to this issue.

Check out this "mega-swing": I vividly recall our first visit to the maternal fetal medicine specialist who I began seeing with my fourth pregnancy. Are you familiar with the "I Survived!" stickers that are often handed out to nauseous folks as they exit the giant roller coasters at amusement parks? Well, after a "work-up" appointment at this clinic, I felt like I had ridden the Scream Machine of Infertility, and I deserved a sticker! Within just a couple of hours at this office, I encountered all of the anguish of believing our baby was gone (after experiencing my most severe, bright red spotting episode in the lab's restroom), and then I ascended to an emotional climax upon seeing the heartbeat of our normal baby via our first ultrasound. Now that's an intense ride. Certainly one to be remembered. Surviving the drastic plummet downward and then the jovial ascent to the top merits much more than a sticker. *(On a lighter note: Let me briefly account to you another memorable aspect of this same appointment – its humorous, yet awkward nature. My general OB had recommended total bedrest during the early stages of this pregnancy. I was in a prone position at all times apart from potty breaks and quick showers. So as I entered this unfamiliar waiting room of my out-of-town specialist, I was very disappointed (yet not surprised) to discover no other person lying on the loveseats awaiting her appointment. Imagine that! I signed in at the front desk and then proceeded to stretch myself out on two adjoining hardback chairs. Here we were ... Rusty upright, Mom upright, lots of pregnant ladies upright and two dozen sets of eyes staring at me, the gal whose matted hair was hidden by a red ball cap – oh and did I mention? I was lying down. It only gets more humiliating from there. We all know the influence of the initial 10 seconds of a first impression. Wonder how that worked for me and my world-renowned lecturing doctor? With dignity, she entered the consultation room, nodded to Rusty and then with a startled gasp acknowledged me lying flat of my back on the commercial tile floor. Her candid reaction clearly revealed I was the first patient who had ever introduced herself while sprawled out on the floor.)*

The whirlwind of the ups and the downs. Within a few weeks of my fourth pregnancy, Rusty and I were once again swept into the inevitable cyclone. The spotting started. After some bloodwork and an ultrasound that showed no baby, my nurse practitioner sent me home, told me to take it easy and wait for the hCG levels to rise. I was to come back within forty-eight hours. If the values doubled we would know things were progressing, and perhaps it was just too early to see the baby via an ultrasound. The baby-less ultrasound images were a low for me, but the text I received from a respected minister became a high. It read: *Kay and I will pray and continue to pray til the birth of this baby.* Til the birth of this baby? I grabbed ahold of that phrase and held on for dear life. A man of God said it. To me, he had basically prophesied a glorious outcome.

Day after day, my faith slowly grew. Yet I was very reluctant. My hCG numbers increased at textbook increments, but with each trip to the restroom my spirits would undoubtedly be hampered. Spotting has that potential. Something as habitual and normal as going to the restroom can quickly take upon the nature of a science project. Rigorous monitoring and speculating begins, and the potential for becoming overwhelmed certainly exists.

I tried to rationalize why God would allow abnormal spotting in this pregnancy. I had witnessed various circumstances which I interpreted as repeated affirmations of a healthy birth. I sought my Heavenly Father, to the best of my ability, trying to discern His purpose. I came to this conclusion: God's intent was for me to have the baby. The spotting was just a bump in the road that was being used to shape me into a more faith-filled person. I would talk through this reasoning in my head and even share it with others from time to time. My journal entry for Thursday, December 17, reads: *Maybe having genuine faith is where God wants to get me in my relationship with Jesus. Perhaps, this entire ordeal of spotting is for God to take me to a new place with Him – a level of faith-filled praying.* That really is all I could figure. I committed to develop a bold, believing faith. If this was God's reason for the temporary "kink" in my pregnancy, I was willing to apply myself and attempt to spiritually "get" what He had for me. I prayed fervently for God to perfect my faith once and for all and give me an Abrahamic faith that would be counted to me as righteousness. I wanted desperately for this early pregnancy spotting to be the instrument which would revolutionize me into an "ask, believe, receive"[1] kind of Christian.

Each day I would "work on" my faith. Overcoming doubt and obtaining true faith became my spiritual project from sun-up to sun-down. I spent most of my days on our couch flat on my back. I'd relish verse after verse in my white hardback Bible. This is not your typical, giant, white, family Bible – the kind Grandmaw won for packing a pew at the 1954 Spring Revival. It doesn't even have a place for the family tree in its front. I just preferred its sturdy cover which made it so much easier to handle as I had to do all of my reading LYING DOWN. I dissected Scriptures related to physical healing, and with everything in me, I would ask believing and envisioning complete healing for my baby and me. I studied Scriptural criteria for healing. On more than one occasion, I welcomed the ministry of "laying on of hands and the anointing of oil." Several times our tiny living room was filled with folks dropping in for prayer, believing and claiming in faith God's remedy.

Every couple of days or so, I was allowed to get up and go out for a doctor's appointment. Those days would have been completely inviting and exciting apart from the possibility of hearing a bad doctor's report. But, with ecstatic thanksgiving, I would receive promising prognoses, and my walls of disbelief began to crumble. Daily I endeavored to develop the type of faith God intended for me, and then the Lord seemed to affirm it. It was somewhat of a cycle: I would pray with believing; a prayer would be answered, and my faith would increase. As my faith grew, my ability to pray with believing became easier. And eventually, I felt like I was becoming more of what the Lord wanted me to be; all the while, my baby and I were being healed. In my mind, the situation never strayed from this belief: God had allowed me to get pregnant; He had promised this child, and the early complications were just His method of transforming me into a forever faith-filled, non-doubting child of His.

The endeavor of growing my faith was personal and private, a matter of prayer and reflection that I focused upon from my prone position as I would look up at the deer mounts which hang above our oversized sofa. But one day I felt a public expression of my faith was required.

Don't you just love it when the Lord tells you to do something that has the potential to humiliate you completely? Do you cringe when you hear His still small voice instructing you to "reach out" in a way that might seem totally strange to the lost world? We just can't seem to get those times out of our minds. I'll never forget a few years back when I *had* to stop at an elderly lady's house, get out of my car, and beg her to release her push mower and let me finish mowing her yard. Her lot sat on a busy road, and as the cars zoomed by, it wouldn't have been that odd looking, except for the fact I was wearing a Sunday dress. You know those kinds of moments I'm talking about. You are trying to go about your normal day, and with complete certainty you know the Lord is prodding you into a ministry action that may cost you a bit of dignity (at least in the world's eyes). You must respond in order to follow your Master, even though you may become the object of some strange looks.

The Lord provided me with such an incident at an OB visit during this fourth pregnancy. God and I had been cultivating my seed of faith (all within the walls of our living room). But on this particular day, I believed He was requiring me to take a stab at *practicing* my faith. I was a few weeks pregnant, and I was *still* spotting. On this day, my faith was running on low, and my doubts were over-flowing. My hCG levels had been drawn at the lab, and I was meeting with my OB nurse. When I got ready to leave, she told me to follow her to get some pre-natal vitamin samples. My response: "I don't need many." It was like my flesh took over, and out came the unbelief (which, by the way, is sin). We walked down to a closet, and she handed me a case of vitamins with six boxes in it. And then, the monster of disbelief struck at full force, and with no resistance it was able to completely seize the moment. I shook my head, handed the case back and said, "Oh, I don't need that many." The situation gets even bleaker; she then handed me *two* boxes, and - can you believe it? – I took *one* of those boxes and handed the *other* back. My hasty response was a huge setback in advancing my faith. I had been in spiritual boot camp for developing my faith, and now my OB nurse demonstrated more belief than I did. With a frustrated look on her face she said, "You're gonna have to be positive."

As I walked out of the clinic with my one-week's-worth of pre-natal vitamin samples, God's Spirit made it very clear that I had *not* exercised my faith. I was heartbroken. I had lost. And my sinful flesh had won. Can't you relate to moments like that where you have failed the Lord and you absolutely hate your *flesh?* I was totally irritated and ashamed of my display of disbelief.

Boy, I really wished I had done better in that hallway. Things would have been much simpler and far-less embarrassing in the long run. You see, my mom was my chauffeur on this trip, and after we got a couple of blocks down the road towards my "baby-on-board-friendly, why bother hot mocha," I informed her we must turn around. I could hear it. It may have been a whisper, but I could, indisputably, hear the no-nonsense voice of my Father speaking to my heart. We *had* to return to the clinic; Mom *had* to drop me off, and I *had* to go to the front sliding window (again) and ask to see my nurse (again). I knew the Lord would have it no other way.

My nurse rounded the corner, with raised eyebrows and with a "what-can-I-do-for-you" look on her face. In order for me to be obedient to my Lord, I explained to her that I had not exercised my faith. I told her I was going to start believing, and I wanted (and needed) those extra vitamins. She must have understood; she graciously smiled and said, "I believe in my heart this one is going to work." She explained that my hCG levels were exactly where they needed to be, and the ultrasound showed exactly what it should have shown. With a hug and a full case of vitamins, she told me she really had a good feeling about this one. Do you see how it was all working? When I was faith-filled, my faith was increased.

Even though a bit of my pride was challenged that day, I *had* to and I wanted to obey the Lord. As I exited the clinic, Mom was rounding the corner in our family's beloved 1987 Suburban. Upon seeing the big 'Burban headed my way, I lifted my full case of vitamins above my head with one hand and pointed at them with the other, mouthing to mom, "I - got - my - vitamins." She pulled up beside me and gave me a little nod as I climbed into the vehicle. The casual expression on her face seemed to say to me, "Yes, Candise, you got your vitamins. Good girl!"

That day was a spiritual milestone for me; I took a leap of faith by re-entering the clinic to retrieve all my vitamins. And with that tiny act of obedience, I claimed my healing. From that point on, I had a certainty of a healthy pregnancy and delivery. After riding a few miles toward home, I sent a text to my closest friends and family. It said, *I BELIEVE!*

Things really began to shape up after my vitamin acquisition. My spotting became minimal, and I was experiencing a full-blown array of pregnancy symptoms. I optimistically welcomed the morning sickness, the frequent (better yet constant) urination, and my expanding waistline.

I was doing what all expectant mothers should do: taking my vitamins, avoiding caffeine, wearing my seatbelt, and forgoing hot baths. I was scheduled for an ultrasound at eight-and-a-half weeks. Rusty, Mom, and I headed to my specialist in Nashville. I don't know what it was about needing Mom to be there. Whether the news was to be bad or good, I wanted her there. Of course, I was a bit nervous. My ultrasound track record wasn't one to "write home about," so imagining the worst was hard for me not to do. At the same time, I was excited. Excited about the possibility of seeing our new life and being told everything was okay.

Rusty had never seen a "good" ultrasound. Usually by the time he made it to an OB appointment, the little flicker of a heartbeat had been stilled. All he had ever been able to see was a lifeless baby or an empty sack. But today's medical movie was destined to be a "Blockbuster." As soon as the technician had everything in place and the screen's images cleared from the movement of positioning the devices, Rusty and I instantly beheld the tiny, yet strong, flashing speck of our sweet baby's heartbeat. There I lay in wonder, completely overtaken by an indescribable love. It truly was the most precious, most beauti-ful moment of my life. I held the strong, yet tender hand of my life's love and became ut-terly overwhelmed. Here we were. Husband and wife ... now seeing through the blur of tears ... for the first time ... our little baby who was created by the greatest bond of human love either of us had ever experienced. Every-thing was absolutely perfect. The dimensions. The heart rate. The implantation. The momma. The baby. Perfect.

> There I lay in wonder, completely overtaken by an indescribable love.

Rusty just couldn't get enough. He looked like the little boy you'd see in the reptile house at the zoo, leaning over the safety barricade, struggling to get a closer look at the cool, giant boa. He was sitting on the edge of his chair, his neck stretched out, his face within a few inches of the monitor. The technician would scan around my uterus, and each time the baby would appear, Rusty would point and say, "There it is." He was completely mesmerized, completely in love, completely in awe. I honestly believe he could have sat there all day waiting for just one more peek at his teeny baby. I, on the other hand, was ready for that lady to get that transducer out of me – before she disturbed the little tot and the nest he or she had made! And besides, there was a whole world of folks outside that tiny ultrasound room who were awaiting our report, and what fun it was going to be broadcasting our news.

Before we got out of the doctor's office, I had sent our miracle baby's photo to scores of folks' cell phones. The subject read: *Jesus is good! Perfect baby and Momma!*

A caption followed: *HUGE Praise Jesus Tailgate Party!*
August 19. Murray Hospital parking lot. Tents, grills,
praise music, snowcones, testimonies. Everyone invited!
Spread the word. Praise Jesus Celebration! Thanks for
continued prayers!

Yes, within just seven short months, I was going to
have this baby! And the masses would be praising Jesus!
How could God have it any other way?

The days after the normal ultrasound were some of the
happiest days of my life and our marriage. The spotting
completely subsided. I was healed! The timing had been
perfect. The fetal maternal specialist said harmless spotting – a result of implantation – normally begins around
five weeks five days. BINGO! I hit that date right on the
head. Such spotting was expected to end around eight
weeks. Yep, I met that deadline, too! The little spotting
phase was over, and I could continue with the next stages
of pregnancy. I believed with all my heart that I had
crossed over the bump in the road, and from here on out,
everything would be perfect.

Mom and I made our first (albeit 10-years overdue) shopping trip for maternity clothes. I finally got to start wearing a "belly belt" I had borrowed from my sister-in-law.
I was back out among the living, getting to go to church
and enjoy what I had never gotten to experience before – a
return to society after a bout with spotting which I had
won! And there couldn't have been a happier girl in all the
world on the night I sported my "baby bump" on a much-
needed date. It was a night complete with Mexican food
(my favorite) and a hand-in-hand stroll through Wal-Mart
with my too-good-to-be-true husband. I had officially entered into life as a pregnant woman who would soon hold
her child in her arms. I had received spiritual and medical
affirmations, and now my body was physically confirming

this pregnancy as it conformed into an incubator where a precious life would grow and form. And from where, in just a few months, our baby would miraculously be birthed.

The evening following our date night, Rusty's mother, who we affectionately call MiMi, decided to get everyone together for supper and fun family times. This would be my first post-spotting family event. I was feeling great, and I couldn't wait for everyone to see how big my belly had gotten. (Now don't get me wrong; I don't want to be misleading. The pooch was definitely there, but a stranger probably wouldn't have recognized it.) I got all "fixed up," and before we left the house, I sent a picture text of my tummy to my faithfully praying friend, Rebecca.

Everyone loves going to MiMi and Papa's house. I had been so nauseated, but when I saw the homemade pizza I was in hog heaven. I was craving the carbs, the dairy, the meat. My former one-a-day salads just weren't working for me. So without hesitation, my plate made a sudden bypass over the greens and such, and soon I was finishing off my third slice of the most delicious and satisfying pizza I had ever eaten. The house was full of laughter, and for once in my life, I was the daughter-in-law who became the obstetricistic's interviewee. All the Farmer ladies – aunts, grandmothers, cousins – sat around the kitchen table and sincerely inquired about my pregnancy progress. As the discussion continued, pregnancy/baby stories were shared by all, and within an hour or so, I had officially been initiated and enlisted as a "Farmer Mother." Finally!

The conversation came to a slight lull, and I left the table for one of my frequent potty breaks. I took about four steps towards the bathroom, and with absolutely no warning whatsoever, I knew something was horribly wrong. There was no pain at all, but I undeniably felt a huge mass pass down through my lower abdomen and then with no resistance make its way out of me. I never broke stride. As I passed Rusty, who was kicked back in the recliner (probably "talking fishing" with his uncle as they watched a rodeo), I said, "Honey, come here." And then, within seconds, the immaculate, humble guest bathroom of my dear in-laws transformed into the setting of a miscarriage nightmare. I had never heard of and still have never heard of such a miscarrying scenario in my life. Literally (and with a respect for being too graphic), blood was slowly pouring out of me absolutely everywhere. The scene was as gory as any "CSI" junky can imagine.

I was trying to take off my boots and jeans, and Rusty was pacing, walking miniature circles with the cordless phone to his head. And MiMi … Mercy … Mimi. For over eighteen years, my mother-in-law has consciously and successfully made an effort to assure me of her love, support and acceptance. But her reaction that night conveyed a degree of compassion for me I had never realized. What my body was doing was beyond my control, and several things needed to be done instantly. Rusty and I responded with some form of action – calling the doctor, getting clothes on for the transport to the ER. We didn't verbalize "you do this," "I'll do this;" we just on our own started to *do* something. And MiMi took action as well. As I struggled with my blood-soaked jeans, MiMi was bent over the toilet and with desperation (but no reservation) was trying to recover some of the clotty matter I had passed. I'll always have within me the image of her beautiful, French-tipped fingers straining through the tinted water and scooping out what could have been the remains of my baby, her grandchild. Apparently, that was her task for the moment, and she was doing what she needed to do.

The ride to the emergency room was intense. My mom and dad met us on the way so Mom could ride with us. Rusty called the sheriff (his hunting buddy and close friend from high school) and told him the route we would be taking. Rusty told the sheriff he would be driving with his flashers on, and he would not be stopping if blue lights tried to pull him over. Sheriff Belew offered to get us an escort, but that would have never worked because Rusty was driving so fast. There was no officer (or NASCAR driver) who could have ever caught up with us. I was lying in the backseat and really had no idea how fast we were going. Rusty admits to 90-plus in spots. The rural two-lane road is extremely curvy and quite frequently becomes the locale for wrecks instigated by darting deer. Somehow (we know the "Somehow") we made it to the ER.

No one had to be told. The amount of blood I had lost and was continuing to lose completely eliminated any-one's projection of the baby. You didn't have to be a doctor or nurse to recognize the baby was not the medical concern at this point. Without any discussion, a common, understood knowledge existed among everyone. There was no baby. Measures were being taking to save the life in jeopardy ... and that was mine. As an attempt to stop the blood loss, I underwent an emergency D & C – this time with a spinal because of my three-piece pizza intake. Around 11 p.m., I was rolled into a single room where I'd stay for the next two-and-a-half days.

Chapter VIII

I'm in a Real Mess Now

I hate pajama pants! Why on earth can't people put on a pair of real pants to go to Wal-Mart? If it is a comfort issue for these folks, there are lots of options. They should try yoga pants, the traditional nylon or cotton sweatpants or even a pair of loose-fitting, worn-out blue jeans. Flannel pants printed with multi-colored flip-flops and with a drawstring for a waistband are attire for in-home lounging. Hot pink, terry cloth pants with "ANGEL" appliquéd in deep purple across the buttock panels are *not* designed to be worn in public. I don't know why, but I've always hated the idea of wearing pants intended as sleepwear to the grocery store and the like ... But on Monday morning, January 11, 2010, I left the Murray-Calloway County Hospital wearing (you guessed it!) pajama pants. No one could have ever mistaken them for anything other than pajamas. Had they been a solid navy or grey, they possibly could have passed for yoga pants, but they were not. My apparel that day consisted of an over-sized T-shirt and a pair of pale pink, plaid, pajama bottoms. The first of many indicators that I was in a real mess!

My body was ragged. I'm sure my systems had no idea what was going on. My reproductive organs had just been disfigured by the sudden and premature removal of a detached fetus. My endocrine system was completely whacked up in an effort to re-adjust hormone levels. My circulatory system was trying to recoup from a battle with low pulse and blood pressure due to the substantial loss of blood. My urological "things" had been tortured with *two* urinary catheters (one inserted as an emergency). My physical body was broken, and although it was dismissed to recover at home, the other *parts* of me remained in critical condition. Anyone around me could see, I belonged in a Trauma Unit for the mentally, spiritually, and emotionally-injured and diseased.

It was a surreal moment for me when I walked back into my house that I had left two days earlier. I entered the living room to find everything as we had left it. The couch was still there ... the one I thought my body was going to grow attached to just a week earlier. The deer on the wall that I had visually examined to the point of knowing the arrangement of each whisker. They were still hanging above the couch. My "pregnancy days' journal" – still on the end table. And there was the white, hard-back Bible – for some reason, I couldn't even look at it.

I was utterly empty and depleted.

I came home with emptiness. I was so worn from it all. I had been pulverized by everything related to this pregnancy, from the double-lined indicator to the medical events of the past weekend. Just about every moment of my life for the past two months had in some way *now* been used to sear me emotionally. The sensory endings of my emotions had been cauterized by all of the ups and downs, and as I sat back down upon our couch, my soul felt nothing. I was utterly empty and depleted. Empty of tears. Empty of faith. Empty of my inner "pep talks." Empty of feeling. Empty of reasoning. Empty of hope. Empty of me.

A couple of days passed, and I knew that physically my body wasn't rebounding as it had in the past. I knew the circumstances of this miscarriage could by no means be compared to the other three "cake walks" I had faced, but still, I could tell I wasn't getting much better. I recognized my slow progress, but honestly, I was too emotionally raw to really care. My prognosis spiritually? Not good. That recovery was even slower.

My white, hardback Bible just sat there. The first day I couldn't even look at it. To me, so much was represented by that book. Actually, my entire existence for the past two months involved that book. Day in and day out, I had wrapped around my heart the comfort of its pages that related to every event of my pregnancy. And now it sat on our ottoman, by itself, untouched. I didn't know what to think of this book. So I let it sit, and I tried not to glance its way.

Within a day or so, I found myself looking at it, being drawn to it. For almost fifty consecutive days, this book had been my closest friend. The majority of my days had been spent reading it. It had become a treasure chest to me, filled with everything I needed for each new day. I had grown to eagerly anticipate opening it; I had started savoring its every word, and with reluctance, I had begun to hesitate before I would set it aside. This white, plain hardbound Bible had been such a huge part of my past two months, and within a few days of my dismissal from the hospital, I began to miss my Bible, miss holding it, miss seeing what it would say to me. My literary companion had been a huge part of my life. It may have been caused by an urge of habit, but one morning I had to pick it up.

The weeks after my now fourth miscarriage were very complicated. Emotionally, I was pretty much "out of the game." Physically, I wasn't doing well, and this medical struggle had me disengaged emotionally and spiritually. I knew, from experience, I could expect some cyclic, hormonal normalcy to resume after four to six weeks. But after six weeks, I was convinced something was wrong. Some of my pregnancy symptoms had subsided, but I knew the ongoing spotting, the lack of a period and the still swollen breasts were not the norm – at least at this point. These "conditions" that seemed to keep hanging around were a red flag to me, and my pursuit of getting them medically fixed replaced my usual tendency to work through the grief of losing another baby. My general OB wasn't sure what was going on, so I had to begin the lengthy and consuming search of finding the right specialist. Finally, after countless visits to a highly-respected internist, a gynecologist oncologist, and a menopause specialist, it was determined that I had an unidentifiable large mass growing within the wall of my uterus. The usually prescribed shots of methantriadone (a form of chemotherapy) and an attempt to surgically remove the mass were not options. The mass was too large for the chemo treatment to be fully effective, and the vascular nature of the mass could cause a fatal hemorrhage, making the removal impossible. I was 38-and-a-half, I had no children, and I was going to have to have a hysterectomy. It was completely conclusive; a team of the South's most respected specialists had scrutinized over my case for weeks, seeing me in their offices every forty-eight hours. There was no way around it ... I was to be incurably barren ... forever.

The loss of our little baby #4 almost went unnoticed, unacknowledged. My near-death experience during the actual miscarriage quickly swept all awareness of our precious baby under an invisible rug. And that is where the memory of (and grief for) our baby remained. The three-and-a-half months following the miscarriage were plagued by my extended illness, prolonged diagnosis, hysterectomy and recovery. All of this, made it impossible for me to deal with a pain that must be emotionally and spiritually addressed.

My health (and life) was at stake. The partial hysterectomy – which I've learned so much through all of this – would leave me without a uterus but with both ovaries. My preferences, my agenda, my concerns no longer mattered. The surgery would take place. And although, I was not ready at all to live my life without a uterus, barren forever, I wanted desperately for the surgery to be scheduled immediately. If there was a cancellation, I wanted it. The doctors had convinced me of the danger of me harboring the mass, and I wanted it out.

Rusty and I went to a surgery scheduling appointment with the surgeon, and we were able to effectively communicate our desire for an A.S.A.P. surgery. It had been four months since I had found out I was pregnant, and there needed to be some finality to the craziness. When we got done with her, she was well-aware that we wanted the very earliest surgery date. Upon returning from her scheduling agent, she informed us of the first opening for an operating room and the availability of the robot that would be performing my surgery. The date – March 30. And be there at 6 a.m.

March 30th. To my surgeon, this was just another day to be spent in the OR. But March 30th meant so much more to me. It was my spiritual birthday. Yes, thirty years earlier, to the date, the Lord drew me to Himself, convicted me of my sinfulness (even at the age of eight, there was plenty of it), and He tenderly called me to become a child of His. His grace had been enough to save me from eternal damnation on March 30, 1980, and I knew without a doubt His grace would see me through this life-altering day. On March 30, 2010, I entered the surgery wing of Baptist Hospital with complete peace. The Lord's kindness and mercy were showered upon me. After a flawless procedure and remarkable recovery, I was discharged the following day. The pathology reports were disease-free. It was determined the large growth was placental tissue, and again, the inevitability of the hysterectomy was affirmed.

Chapter IX

Now for Life without a Uterus

I survived! And that's just about all I could say for myself. I hadn't really come through with flying colors, but I had come through. It was almost six months after our fourth child was conceived when I gloriously got dismissed from the care of my gynecological specializing doctors. It was over. I was well again. Finally. And Praise the Lord!

Constant attention had been given to my physical condition for six months. From my first sign of spotting on "Week Five Day Five" to my surgery follow-up appointment, scores of folks had fixated upon my health. Doctors had. Family had. Friends had. And I had. During those months, I totally had neglected the nasty, open-wound that gaped within my heart. I lost my baby, and that was huge!

The magnitude of this final miscarriage could not remotely be compared to our other losses. My degree of affection for this child was no greater than it was for the others, but it was the exceptional details related to and the overall nature of this pregnancy that powered the knock-out blow to my soul. Losing this particular baby was incredibly complicated from many perspectives, and the realization that our "August 19 Tailgate Party" was indefinitely postponed shook me to my very core. Never in my life, had my stability, sanity and spirituality been challenged as it was upon my heart grasping the fact that, once again, we were in need of no nursery.

It was an early morning in May when I was abruptly awakened by enemy fire. The attack was unexpected, and unfortunately, I had allowed the enemy of my mind to enclose upon my heart's vital territory. With almost no warning of an attack, I found myself huddled on our sofa, alone, in the wee hours of the morning, crying. The missile that had been launched months earlier had traveled its course and now its pre-determined target was in sight. My faith and emotions were under an assault. The bomb of awareness struck with undiscriminating placement and monumental force. My heart had been hit! I was barren forever, and there on our sofa, I fully absorbed the impact and aftershock of this reality.

Where had I been for the past four months? Why had I left my heart so unguarded and vulnerable?

Where had I been for the past four months? Why had I left my heart so unguarded and vulnerable? Perhaps it was the preoccupation with my physical health. That's all I can attribute it to. However, this particular morning my emotions and spirituality had been left totally exposed, and a part of me was taken captive by my greatest enemy.

Through tears I watched the clock, and when I suspected my lone sister-in-infertility (in another time zone) was awake, I gave her a call. Rebecca answered the phone with a cheerful, "Hey, girl" maybe trying to disguise the fact that I had woken her up. I'm not sure of my response, but the next thing I remember her saying is "It's hit you; hasn't it?" She knew it was inescapable. At some point I was going to have to deal with the outcome of my reproductive life. And this outcome? *It had hit me.* There would be no outcome.

I felt as if I had been abandoned. I was now left completely alone. I would be the only woman left without her baby. My existence became overcome with the following mindset: *Every* well-known Biblical account of infertility ends with a reproductive success. *Every* memoir in the contemporary "empty cradle" books tells of a long-awaited miracle baby, and *every* woman (albeit just two) in my community who I knew of having multiple miscarriages eventually delivered their healthy "bundle of joy." *Every* woman, that is, except for me. How had I ended up like this? Why didn't I do something to keep this from happening? I would never have a child, and I knew of no other woman in this same predicament. Yes, I was aware of two or three ladies who have no children, but I just assumed they had never wanted any. And I'm not sure where my reasoning got this perspective – but I also supposed that if they *had* wanted a baby, their desire was minimal in comparison to mine. This assumption only made me feel more isolated. Many times barrenness was placed upon a woman in the Bible as a curse of God. And as my fleshly thinking relentlessly fired upon me that May morning, I felt as if I had been cursed, cursed by God, and I didn't hesitate to tell Rebecca my conclusion during my meltdown.

So I became childless forever, and I was without a clue of what to do. I was completely at a loss of how to live with this "condition." No one was qualified now to teach me the barrenness "tricks of the trade." My dentist's wife could have related with her four miscarriages, but with the birth of their three healthy children, our "common ground" lost its surety. My momma couldn't tell me how she worked through her life of childlessness – which she never had to encounter (duh! thank goodness!). My friend Rebecca had been able to walk with me through every facet of my infertility, but now her ability to relate had met its end. And as hard as I tried, the account of an incurably-barren "Sarah" could not be found within the pages of my Bible. I was alone ... more alone than I had ever been before!

Any bridges that had existed between other infertile women and me were being burned one by one. And to complicate the matter ... my faith was teetering on the hope spotlighted in a hymn I had sung of all my life. I *had* built my hope on the Solid Rock of Christ. But the loss of our fourth baby and the guarantee of a childless future left me on sinking sand.

"This just doesn't make sense – why God would do all of this."

Five weeks (and five days) into my fourth pregnancy, Rusty uttered these words as we made our way to the OB upon me starting to spot – again! Please understand that Rusty is a very deliberate person; he honestly thinks through every word he says. So when he made this candid, sincere comment, I knew that it was not just a careless "slip of the tongue." Rusty truly was puzzled. To him, it did not make sense for me to be losing another baby especially considering all of the unique confirmations the Lord seemed to have been granting us. Rusty knew what he was saying that morning as he drove us to the clinic, and I'm not sure if it was the level of his confusion or his courage, but somehow he managed to let the words out. His single, heartfelt comment seemed to become a theme for the several months to follow ... and only he had had the "guts" to *say* what was in his heart.

You understand where I'm coming from; don't you? Do you ever find yourself wanting to think something, but then your reverence for the Lord "kicks in" and you deliberately rid your mind of that ideal? **II Corinthians 10:5** states, **"We are destroying speculations and every lofty thing raised up against the knowledge of God, and we are taking every thought captive to the obedience of Christ."**[1] Perhaps it is our awareness of this admonition that prompts us to rid from our thinking any Godless notions. Sometimes we don't consciously process the steps within this tendency, but regardless, there are some thoughts that we dare not entertain, much less verbalize. It is our fear of and respect for the Lord that stifles such speculations and discourages them from being spoken.

Consider this sea-faring Englishman's historical statement. "Not even God, Himself, can sink this ship."[2] Does that statement give you the chills? I've often wondered ... Would the Titanic still be afloat today, providing luxurious cruises for vacation seekers? Is it possible the mammoth, ancient cruise liner would still be at sea if a self-claimed nautical "engineer" had not *thought* and then *verbalized* his scientific projection? Did the proud mental notions of a mortal employee of the White Star Line make the Lord angry? When God Almighty heard the comment that traveled to every continent, "Not even God Himself can sink this ship," was this boat Divinely destined to sink? I do not know. But, I do know that I have allowed certain limits (whether they be from my bondage of carnality or from

God) to constrain my thinking. There are some thoughts I do not give myself permission to ponder, and there are certainly some ideologies I feel I must never verbalize.

Psalms 94:11 — "The Lord knows the thoughts of man;"

I am fully aware that God knows my every thought, as stated in **Psalms 94:11: "The Lord knows the thoughts of man;"**[3] He understands all of my thoughts much better than I understand them. I recognize that He comprehends my tiniest notion before it is actually formulated within my mind. But for some reason (and I'm sure it is my carnality and complex human nature), I've been playing in an innocent mind game for years. Here's the "little" inclination I have come to accept for myself ... if ever a thought of mine indicates to God I am ungrateful or second-guessing His doings, I want that thought – whatever it may be – to be completely cast from me ... way, way, far away from me. I don't want to be remotely associated with such a thought. I truly believe I am the most blessed person in the entire world. I fully acknowledge the mercies of God being poured out upon the lives of me and my family. With no uncertainty at all, I am persuaded that I am a recipient of God's sweetest blessings, and my heart is genuinely grateful for His merciful provision upon my life. But after acknowledging my incurable barrenness, my peon intellect began to hear the faint whispers coming from fleshly thinking and the eternal foe of my heart. I began to struggle with another mind game – one that was completely foreign to me. I did not want to make any statement (or even mentally consider one), as genuine and true as it may be, that would bring God's ship-sinking wrath upon my life.

But, in all honesty, Rusty was not alone in his thinking. It made no sense to me either – "why God would do all of this." I could not identify any reasoning for me to lose another baby and to bear the label of "barren for life." And even though I was way too fearful to state it, I also agreed with Rusty, in that, God was the instigator behind this tragedy and hopeless biological condition. To me, my miscarriage and hysterectomy were all completely senseless (and dare I say, cruel?). I was scared to death (literally) to articulate my bewilderment, and I desperately tried to barricade such harsh assumptions from my mind. But they were there ... and God knew them.

Chapter X

A Place I Never Wanted to Be

My white, hard-back Bible. All books are meant to be read. Wouldn't you agree? But my participation in the #1 Best-Seller's Book Club was off to a slow start. Aesop's tortoise had nothing on me. Upon returning home from my emergency D & C, it literally took almost 48 hours for my reluctant hands to pick up God's Word. And then I remember, just sitting with it; I held the hard-bound copy in both hands, just staring at its simple cover. "The Holy Bible." The book that had "come to life" for me during the past months, providing me much company, encouragement, and faith. I was only able to hold it at this point. I felt forsaken, almost misled. Lied to? No way, that was too scary for me to even contemplate. My incredibly sluggish pace was set ... I had glanced at the holy book as it sat upon our ottoman ... I had intention-ally looked at the unopened, sacred manuscript ... I had approached it ... grasped it ... maintained my grip as I sat down ... I had stared at its closed cover. This first leg of my Bible-reading pursuit took days. My linger-ing strides continued for weeks. My communion with the Lord seemed hampered and stifled. I couldn't talk to

Him (at least not like I used to), and the words from His Holy Book were finding it difficult to permeate my soul. Something strange, a totally new dynamic between my Lord and me existed. I didn't like it at all. It frightened me, and I needed for this unfamiliar barrier to go away.

I hate pajama pants, but I LOVE youth camp! Some folks can't stand being around teenagers. After all, aren't all adolescents obnoxious and punky? Why would any 30-something-year-old couple want to spend five days with the brats that some folks label as *ungrateful and rebellious*? Well, I can't answer that for you, but there is this unexplainable passion within Rusty and me. We just can't help it; we are undeniably wild about the reckless generation that so many people cannot tolerate. And the highlight of our lives each summer is our week spent at youth camp.

The July following my hysterectomy in March, Rusty and I found ourselves loading a charter bus with 50-plus teenagers and a handful of adult chaperons. Our destination – Lake Williamson in Carlinsville, Illinois. And if we could manage to get there in spite of being high-jacked by a fog of body odor and the constant "yah yah-ing" of two dozen teenaged-girls, it would be a miracle. Thankfully, we arrived intact, and the week of fun began.

My body was 100%. Physically, I felt as strong as ever. I conquered the "Monster Zipline" that raced me over Lake Williamson and then dumped me into its refreshing water. I ascended the inflatable "IceBerg" in record time, leaving a passel of disbelieving high school students at its base. I fearlessly rode the "Giant Water Slide" which required that I wear a helmet! And the floating "Blob" should have been advertised as a kiddie ride after I gave it a try. I was back! I was almost 40-years-old (really just 39 years and 1 month), and even though the past months had wreaked havoc upon my body, I was still in the game. I was so grateful to be alive. I played like never before. On the outside it appeared that I had finally made a full-recovery, but my spirit was still critically wounded. I was at a place I had never wanted to be. In all honesty, it mattered very little that what I was feeling had never been verbalized. My spiritual mentality had been twisted by my fleshly presumptions and the forces of evil that war against every believer of Christ. My thinking (as un-stated as it remained) had evolved from a trace of doubts concerning God's goodness to an overbearing warped state of bitterness. Eventually, true repentance was of-fered and restoration was received, but nonetheless and regretfully, this dialogue was within my crushed heart ...

How could God do this to me? I am His daughter; right? Well, this is not what Daddies do to their baby girls. My earthly father loves me so much, and he would never let such pain enter my life. He would do everything possible to keep me from hurting like this. And my dad would certainly never be the source of such anguish. This is not what a real dad does. Not a dad who loves his child. I'm so disappointed that my spiritual dad has let me down. And how could He lie to me like this? That's so cruel – to take a little child, fill his/her life with hopeful anticipations and then renege on all of them? Give me a break. That's awful! Why lead me to believe my mother's supernatural drive-way prophecy would come true? Why have me sit on the couch for two-consecutive nights and watch in silence as my husband – who's never read a book outside of the Bible – engrosses himself in a parenting book when we're on the verge of discovering a baby is on board? Why let my nurse practitioner lead me on like she did? Why couldn't God *have just shut her mouth (and the mouths of other doctors and even men of God) before everyone blabbed about how certain it was I would deliver **this** child? Come on. That's mean! I was foolish. I should have never gotten my hopes up. It just makes no sense to take a gal on a joyride of hope and then watch her fall to her emotional doom. And this is not only about losing the baby and being eternally unable to ever have a child. It's also about some other details. Why couldn't it all have been a bit more humane? Not one, but two catheters during my D & C hospital stay? And the post-miscarriage infection? I'd never had one of those before. What's up with that?*

In a nutshell, here is what was happening within my weak mind and spirit ... For thirty years, I had been studying and formulating a mindset about the nature of God ... and now, what I had perceived to be His character for years was being challenged by Him allowing my miscarriage and state of irreversible barrenness. My frailness was processing these tragic events as going against all I had ever believed about God. I was trying, trying to ward off such bitter thoughts about the Lord's involvement, but they were surfacing and re-surfacing within my heart – whether I wanted to admit it or not.

Can't you relate, dear friend? It's hard to admit; isn't it? Doesn't it scare you to acknowledge that you've shaken your fist in the face of Almighty God? Don't you find yourself fearfully looking back upon those moments when you have questioned the will of God? But as hard as you (and I) try to deny it, those doubtful encounters with the Lord are there. Your mind has begun to fantasize about your conception possibilities and your heart has begun to adore the baby growing within you – and if ever, if ever, these dreams have been crushed or the tiny life has been taken from you, there has been a substantial jolt to your spirit and soul. To some degree (hopefully not as astronomical as mine), your faith has wavered and you've questioned God and His intentions. Infertility and pregnancy loss will issue an inevitable crisis of faith. You may have been able to resolve your uncertainties within just a couple of hours during a sleepless night; you may have found your sufficient answers during a series of counseling sessions, or you may have been like me, and you "wollered" quite some time in a pit before latching onto a supernatural wench that pulled you to your peace. And, perhaps, your faith in God is still being tested within the storm's eye. Are you currently wrestling with the skepticism? Are you trying out your newly-developed perspective of God, checking to see if it really fits Him? If that's you, hurting one, prepare yourself. Once again, God's Word is capable of settling your heart's debate.

Green Pastures of a Barren Land

Chapter XI

Principle Four: When Facing a Crisis of Faith, Be Assured – He is the Right Savior!

The room was large, dimly-lit, with open-rafters revealing duct work and wiring. The fog from smoke-machines had filled the stage. The mosh-pit of screaming teenagers had dissipated, and hundreds of students were returning to their seats and opening their Bibles. It was the Tuesday night service of YOUTH ALIVE 2010. I was a chaperon, sitting with all the other chaperons. I was tired from the day of play, and I was being coaxed by the air-conditioning and low-lighting into a restful state with a short nap in my sights. I had not come to the camp with an anticipation of a personal, spiritual renewal. It had been about four months since I entered the ring of skepticism, and I was growing accustomed to my stagnant, cold relationship with the Lord. But in His predictably-unpredictable fashion, the Lord, my Sweet Jesus, miraculously brought to me a much-needed resolution for my troubled soul.

Infertility can alter every aspect of a life. Wouldn't you agree? Think about it. Isn't it crazy how a desire to have a child can consume your ever-waking moment? At one time (and not too long ago), we were all happy, *normal,* newly-wed wives; we just did the ordinary things in life – folded laundry, grocery shopped, cleaned house, went to our ladies' Bible study, had other couples over for dinner, cut out coupons. Things were simple. But upon being whisked away against our wills to the foreign and destitute land of infertility, our total existence on planet Earth was altered.

Now, we are weird. We now do bizarre things – we start off every day *precisely* with a recording of our body temperature, we send our husbands on mid-night runs to the pharmacy to buy ovulation predictor kits, we strategically obligate ourselves to carry *Aunt Josie* to the beauty shop so we can forgo another baby shower, we drive hundreds of miles to doctor's appointments knowing we will forfeit our remaining dignity, and we wear sunglasses *a lot!* But, without a doubt, the most profound – and unpleasant – effect of my reproductive troubles came within a spiritual form. My crisis of faith.

Are you there, dear sister? Are you finding yourself unable to handle the demands of your infertility? Maybe you've gotten most of it all down pat by now ... the labs, the stirrups, the Pampers commercials. But have you still not been able to "work out" your infertility with the Lord? Have the negative pregnancy tests and lifeless ultrasounds distorted your perception of God? Has the pain of your infertility adjusted (or shall I say, *mal*adjusted?) your relationship with the Lord? Is there a twinge of doubt, disappointment and distance between your Creator and you? Whether you've articulately acknowledged

> The violent quakes of doubt that seem to be shattering the foundation of your faith must subside.

118

your spiritual dilemma or whether you have not, makes no difference. If your faith is being shaken by the ruthlessness of infertility (as mine was), fret no more, my friend. There is a solace for your soul. The violent quakes of doubt that seem to be shattering the foundation of your faith must subside. It was the power of God's Holy Word that brought my spirit a glorious stillness that Tuesday night during YOUTH ALIVE 2010. Won't you look with me now at a God-inspired passage that is able to still your trembling soul as well?

In jail for preaching? That doesn't seem fair. God calls a man while he is still within his mother's womb to preach repentance, and then the obedient Gospel-deliverer ends up in prison? That's tough. But, think about it. Isn't that the life story of John the Baptist? We all picture in our minds the same guy. John the Baptist – a wooly dude, skin *kinda* tinted by his bath-less nights in the wilderness, all wrapped up in camel-skin duds, a leather tied belt, a crooked, knotted staff. Rugged to the core. Loud. Maybe obnoxious. He seems a bit misplaced in our world. In today's terms of holy men and women, John the Baptist would certainly be among the radicals. Radical in every way – his faith, his appearance, his diet, his ministry methods. The Bible says that his was the **"voice of one crying in the wilderness" (Matt. 3:3)**[1] His outreach techniques would probably be frowned upon by our 21st century seminary hermeneutics professors. Yet from the sixth month of being in his mother's womb, the world-changing man of God, also known to be Jesus' second cousin, revolutionized his culture – and our entire planet – for the cause of Christ. He heralded the coming of the long-awaited Messiah and called his community (and ultimately all humanity) to repentance. The Lamb of God, whose way had been prepared, said of his forerunner, **"Verily I say unto you, Among them that are born**

of women there hath not risen a greater than John
the Baptist . . .**" (Matt. 11:11)** With no doubt about it,
the fearless messenger of the Lord – once a miracle baby
wrought into the lives of a couple **"well stricken in
years"**[2] – fulfilled his life's purpose; the epistle of Matthew accounts for **"people from Jerusalem and from
all over the Jordan Valley, and, in fact, from every
section of Judea"** coming out to the wilderness to hear
him preach. The masses confessed their sins, and then
they were baptized by John in the Jordan River. **(Matt.
3:5-6)**[3] John the Baptist accomplished his holy mission.

Any of you gals like sports? Oh sure, there has to be
a few of you who spent a day or two on the hardwood
of your alma mater's gym. Surely some of you are still
hanging onto the tarnishing, dust-covered trophies
from your soccer glory days of the nineties. And there
must be a handful among you ladies who can't seem
to discard the old, sweat-stained visor you wore while
playing third base. Sports – they aren't for everyone,
but it's likely, most of us have tried our hand at some
sort of athletic competition.

Team sports got me. My poor mom and dad. Every
night of every week it was something. A game. A practice.
A booster club meeting. It seemed constant. Many times
during the summer months, our family considered setting up a few tents at the ball park and relocating until
the season was over. (Important note: My brother and I
were *very* involved in athletics, but if folks wanted to see
a mama bear come out of her den with vengeance, all they
had to do was schedule a game or practice on a Sunday
or Wednesday night. Thankfully, my parents made tough
decisions for Jon Paul and me; going to church supersed-
ed any commitment at a gym or ball park – at least for
my family.)

You know how it is to be on a team, to have practiced, to have run your legs off, to have spent hours under the security light trying to perfect your free throw, to have attended camps and clinics to develop your fastpitch – that's just what we did when we were young and we so needed the discipline and affirmation that comes with being on a ball team. My philosophy as a big, bad (get this ...) *middle-school* soccer "sweeper" was – if I was going to commit to the time and energy of being on the team, I was going to be on the field! So with that mindset, I practiced and played extra hard. There always has to be a second string and "backup players," but I wasn't going to be one of those.

Can any of you relate? There might not have been an abundance of ability, but the drive was there, and you secured your spot *in* the game. And nothing, absolutely nothing was as maddening to you as being on the court, playing your heart out, hearing the stands erupt as you contribute your share of assists and points, and then ... then turn to hear your coach yelling from the sidelines, seeing him motioning you to your seat on the bench, while swatting your replacement on the shoulder, or fanny, as she entered the game. Are you with me on that? How frustrating to be "in your groove," playing like a champ, and then be jerked from the game to find your front row seat on the pine. It's just no fun *watching* as the other players on your team secure a victory.

Riding the pine. Now if this phrase is unfamiliar to any of you gals, just go on into the den, tap your husband on the shoulder, – being careful not to make him spill his bucket of Cheetos and mug of Diet Coke – momentarily interrupt his Monday night football mania and ask him what "riding the pines" means. He will know. (However, if it is fourth and one in his televised game, don't continue your research.) "Riding the pine" is what all serious athletes hate – it is having to sit the bench. As the world of ministry whirled about him, as Bible study upon Bible study was being conducted, as another revival extended through the weekend and as a revved-up mission team left for its spiritually-impoverished destination – John the Baptist was riding the pine.

Matthew Chapter 11 portrays mankind's Savior and his twelve followers busying about, intently doing the work of the Father. Jesus met with the twelve, commissioned them for ministry, and then they dispersed with Jesus fulfilling his traveling-preaching itinerary. All the while, the founder/president of "New Testament Ministries, Inc." (and the official baptizer of Jesus Christ) sat in prison.

Think through this with me. John had surrendered himself, all of who he was, with reckless abandonment to the calling of his spiritual Father. He had selflessly put all of his energy and existence into announcing Christ's coming. He had practiced hard, and he had played hard. He was getting the job done for the cause of Christ, and then the summons from the sideline could be heard. God withdrew him from the game, and perhaps with little explanation, the Master Life-Coach sat him on the bench. Just as the contest was getting heated, just as the world's top-players committed to play, just as the long-awaited Coach arrived and took over the team ... when everything was "getting good," John was removed from the playing court (if you will). We can only speculate, but is it possible that John had some thoughts like this? ... *Just where have all of these superstars been when I was out there in that wilderness alone? When the entire village thought I had gone nuts? God, you told me to cry out your message, and I did! Nobody wanted to hear Your message, but I shouted it anyway. And that day the Pharisees got after me – I stood up to them for You. Everything I did was for Jesus; people needed to get ready for Him. I thought I was doing a good job. I know all those folks I baptized really believed. I thought You were all in my ministry, Lord. That whole baptizing thing with Jesus ... I didn't think I should have baptized Him, but He insisted. It just seemed everything was going so good. And now, look at me. I thought I'd be out of this dungeon by now. What's going on out there, Lord? Why can't I get out of here? I need to be out there helping them boys of Zebedee's and that tax collector-boy who has all those friends who don't believe. This makes no sense – why you would do all of this. Get me out of here!*

And then the days became weeks, and the weeks became months. What started as an overnight stay in the slammer slowly evolved into an endless nightmare of restraint, confinement, loneliness, and desperation. Doesn't that sound so much like our encounters with infertility? We confront our first miscarriage head-on, assuming it will just be a minor hardship that couldn't possibly alter more than a couple of months of our lives. And then the next thing we know we are sitting in an endocrinologist's office eight years later, completely battered and still childless. Our doubts concerning the instigator of our reproductive challenges arise. None of it makes sense.

The hustle and bustle of reaching the multitudes for Christ had continued in full force within Matthew's Gospel account. Verse two of chapter eleven states that John the Baptist, **while in prison**, heard of all the miracles of the Messiah. Man! Can't you imagine? Did his brow bead up with sweat every time he heard an eruption from the ecstatic crowd? Did his feet become restless when the gym floor rumbled with celebrating fans? Did his rugged hands instinctively begin to roll up his weathered sleeves as reports of an unstoppable drive reached his chamber? Just *hearing* the report from his team, hearing of their success and certain victory – just *hearing* of the "works of Christ"[4] might have made him antsy. Perhaps he began to shuffle within his cell; his heart beginning to race. He wanted in the game! But never did the Coach glance his way. The game seemed to have captured the eyes of *everyone* – even the Coach. And John may have begun to wonder, *Does He even see me down here? I gave my all for Him and for this team. Maybe the whole team and this Coach really aren't all they're cracked up to be? I've been played, alright.*

Please don't overlook the significance of this profound spiritual struggle within the soul of the greatest mortal man born of woman. John the Baptist, the **"prophet of the Most High"** who was ordained by God to **"give knowledge of salvation unto his people, . . . to give a light to those that sit in darkness, . . . and to guide our feet into the way of peace" (Luke 1:76-79)[5]**, doubted God. The perplexing circumstances of his life led him to a path of spiritual disbelief and skepticism. Being jerked from the game (in which he was playing masterfully, by the way) and being shoved to the pine of inhumane imprisonment brought to this world-changing man of God a crisis of faith.

Do you get this? You may have had no success at finding an account of an eternally barren woman in the Bible, but this passage is a sure answer for you! Just as you've questioned the Lord, His goodness, His very nature – the prophet who baptized the incarnate God of this universe, he, too questioned the Lord. Don't you find comfort in that? It is okay! Your reservations, your cynicism, the uncertainty of your faith is common to man and not just any man. It was common to John the

Baptist. And guess what? Even *after* John struggled with his thoughts of disbelief – which could have been laced with bitterness and anger – Jesus Christ still said of him, he was "more than a prophet" and the "greatest among men."[6]

John couldn't stand it any longer. It could have been feelings of betrayal, loneliness, or confusion that prompted him to call for a couple of his disciples. His hopeless imprisonment, which had no end in sight, was no longer his most significant problem. Now, after accepting the irreversible nature of his detention, it is possible his prominent concern became the presence of the distressing dialogue within his heart – a dialogue that was attempting to undermine all he had ever known of the God who had begotten the Savior of the world. What John feared and hated most about his life may have become the uncertainty and instability of his shaking and swaying faith that had, at one time, been so real and reliable that it led to his arrest.

We get that way in our infertility; don't we? There comes a time and point when the prospect of having a child almost becomes secondary. During the initial diagnoses and treatments of our barrenness, our main objective is to have a baby; not having a child is the most unsatisfying factor in our lives. With all certainty, our biggest regret and our main source of discontentment is us not being able to hold the child we so desperately want. That is how the process begins and continues for quite some time. But then, as we continue on and on and on down the desolate road of childlessness, our main disgruntlement is altered a bit. Yes, we, still more than anything, want our infertility to be overcome with the birth of little "Jesse," but what troubles us most, especially we who have a "history" with the Lord, is the undeniable appearance of what seems to be a betrayal from the ultimate Life Giver.

After a decade of miscarriages and heartbreak, my primary complaint transitioned from the disappointment of an empty nursery to the disgust and misery of believing I had been misled in my faith. In the end, I knew I did not *have* to have a baby to survive life with sanity. I completely recognized that a child could add an indescribable amount of fulfillment to my life, but I also was convinced that never could an offspring provide for me the supernatural strength and indescribable peace I would need in order to live the remaining portion of my life on earth. I had surrendered to the fact that life is demanding, and I am weak. As wonderful as being a mother would be, my greatest need was the accessibility to and daily dependence upon an all-powerful God. I could somehow make it without a baby, but my life (at least the quality of it) would be terminated without the presence of God. So, when my infertility extended into years that totaled more than one-third of my age, I became a bit like John the Baptist. The imprisonment of childlessness was, at this point, not the main source of my misery; what troubled me most was the belief I had acquired from my soul's enemy and my fleshly thinking. I had grown to believe that my Forever-Friend of 30 years had forsaken me and that His agenda which I had presumed to be one of hope and blessing had been thwarted. I felt His plan for my life was unreliable and surely could not be trusted. Yikes!

The plot of Matthew Chapter 11 thickens. John the Baptist requests a visit from a couple of his followers, and sure enough the two unnamed disciples showed up for "inmate visitation hours." Perhaps the two visitors obtained their "Visitor" lanyards, withstood the awkward pat-downs, and then entered the penitentiary's day room. And then enters, the aged Baptizer, flanked by two impatient, grimacing guards. Simultaneously, their eyes meet. The imprisoned, John the Baptist, and his two disciples.

Three followers of the Nazarene – three devout men who had chosen a life that required them to daily count the cost. With a glance, the two outsiders could detect John's desperation; his countenance said it all. It had all finally gotten to him. He had seemed so upbeat, so optimistic … up until now. But this time, as the Messiah's forerunner approached, the first signs of despair were easily recognized. John's gait – shuffling and stooped. His ratty beard – unkept and discolored. His dark eyes – now vacant and dull. It was obvious; since their last visit, John had been shackled to his fiercest adversary. He couldn't escape the constant discourse within his feeble heart. The voice of doubt had taken its toll.

Breathless. Deliberate. With sheer exertion, John stutters, "Go ask Him … I've got to … got to know … Would you ask Him for me? … Is He really the One? … the One we've been … waiting for? … Or should we keep on looking?"[7] He did it! Although it took every ounce of what was left of his assaulted spirit, John the Baptist acknowledged his faith's crisis by verbally extending a weary hand of doubt in hopes of being able to grasp onto something, something that could pull him to a fragment of belief. After three-and-a-half months of sitting in a dark prison,[8] seeming to be ignored by the Coach of all creation, John the Baptist was wondering if this whole "Jesus deal" was for real. The disappointment and hardship of imprisonment had left John's faith wavering. Likely, his prominent doubt was not concerning the identity of the Savior, but perhaps his biggest source of bewilderment was directed toward the workings of the Savior. Was this Galilean miracle man's "kingdom" really all He claimed it to be? Could His promise of deliverance and judgment be trusted? Would the turmoil all be ended by Jesus proving Himself to be the Messiah, the Savior, the One worthy of his trust and the lordship of his life?

And sitting there that night in the auditorium of the Lake Williamson Retreat Center, I realized my faith had been asking the same question for the past six months. In spite of a lifetime filled with the richest blessings known to anyone, my journey through infertility had left me wondering, *Had I goofed? Had I placed my trust and life in the hands of the wrong man? The wrong god? Had I been wrong about this "Jesus thing" all along?*

Sweet sister, your crisis of belief is inevitable. Either you are presently in the doubtful turmoil, you are just entering the darkness of disbelief, or perhaps you've just been the recipient of a Divine enlightenment that confirmed your faith in a Sovereign God. Whatever your current case may be, infertility can leave your faith trembling with cynicism. Losing your baby, failing in attempts to conceive, and being faced with the possibility of never sharing your life as a parent – all have the potential to leave you questioning the goodness and love of your Maker. It may not have been a reproductive hardship that drove John the Baptist to question the Lord, but God, in His mercy, graciously included John's faithless dilemma in His Holy Book. And I just can't help but believe it was the all-knowing nature of our Lord that compelled Him to record such an account – an account of a fellow-believer being rescued from his faith's moment of doubt.

Upon hearing of his incarcerated cousin's refutation of faith, Jesus responded with a holy text recorded by Isaiah the prophet – words that John the Baptist had likely been quoting since he was 13 or 14 years old. **"Go and report to John what you hear and see; the BLIND RECEIVE SIGHT and the lame walk, the lepers are cleansed and the deaf hear, the dead are raised up, and the POOR HAVE THE GOSPEL PREACHED TO THEM. And blessed is he who does not take offense**

at Me"[9] (or "to doubt or distrust me" as defined by the original term *skandalizo*)[10] **(Matthew 11:4-6).** Jesus' response was the perfect remedy for John's unstable faith. With words of compassion and a reference to the life-giving Scriptures which had been a certain reality of John's childhood, Christ's assurance was exactly what John needed to hear. The controversial man claiming to have been sent from Heaven (and whose call to allegiance had cost John his freedom) truly was the sin-bearing Christ, completely in control of all of life's circumstances and dependably committed to His followers.

And for me, this is what I heard my Savior say through this His declaration that Tuesday evening ... "Candise, my baby girl, you got it right! It is all over. Leave your doubts behind. You are in a prison, a prison to a condition beyond your control. You're here, and there is no baby in store for you. But I am here! The driveway promise is being fulfilled; I am taking care of your 'baby issue.' And don't you ever doubt – the God in which you placed your child-like faith as a vulnerable eight year-old-girl that glorious morning in March of 1980 – I'm still that God. You made no mistake. I am your Savior, the Savior of the world. Have no doubt about it; you placed your life in the hands of the right One. I'm here to bear your sins and break what is breaking you. My Kingdom is alive and well even though you cannot see it right now. And I have not forgotten or forsaken you, my daughter ... " And by the supernatural, miracle-working power of God's Holy Word, I began to let Truth lead me back to trust. My soul had found its resting place.

Whew! In my heart of hearts that was exactly what I was hoping to hear. It was like a huge relief came over me. I wanted what I had believed about the Lord for so many years to be true, all true. The kind Jesus of whom I had learned in Bible School – I loved Him. The strong

God whom I had watched perform miracles – I needed Him. And my Abba Father who knew me best and loved me most – I had to have Him. Jesus and me, my Lord and me – it had all been for real. Even though He had never left me, He was back.

Take it in, troubled one. Please let the voice of the Lord who loves you more than you can imagine chase your skepticism away. Your enemy's plan is to crush your spirit with the pain of your infertility. He wants nothing more than for your barrenness to wipe you out completely for the cause of Christ. He seeks a spiritual fatality. Don't go there with him. When your moment (or decade) of doubt begins to overtake you, please stop to listen to the words of your Suffering Servant. All of the miracles of which you've heard are true. The Bread of Life's promises upon which you've lived have been fulfilled. Jesus is in control of it all. He has conquered the sin of the world; The Good News of salvation is for everyone. He is all you've ever believed Him to be – the true Savior of your soul. Now walk away from your doubting, and as you turn and go, take to heart Christ's final request issued to John the Baptist's two message-bearing disciples . . . **"Then give him** (in our case, *her*) **this message, 'Blessed are those who don't doubt me.'"**[11]

Principle One: Life is from God (and barrenness is too).

Principle Two: The Lord brought infertility into your life for His glory.

Principle Three: The Lord brought infertility into your life for your good.

Principle Four: When facing a crisis of faith, be assured – He is the right Savior!

Chapter XII

Through Hell and Half the State of Georgia

Oh, how I pray for you – that you are beginning to welcome the mending of your broken spirit. As I began to daily acknowledge that God, in His Sovereignty, "picked me" for the journey of barrenness, ... and that He lovingly intended for my infertility to be for His glory and for my good, ... and that, in spite of my Enemy's usual tactics to inflict disbelief, I *had* placed my faith in the true Savior, ... as I began to "*live*" within these realizations, a stillness and acceptance of my circumstances overtook my heart. I began to heal. Slowly, but surely, I began to "live with" my barrenness. And although, I still wasn't gleefully jumping up and down in excitement as I opened my life's door to this monster, I was beginning to be able to welcome infertility into my existence. As I *received* this disappointing situation into my life, an indescribable peace escorted the barrenness through my heart's opened door. Four, simple, yet incredibly profound, principles of God's Word began to liberate my spirit. Please, my friend, let the power of God's Word renew your faith and restore your broken heart. I plead with you; reflect upon these truths. Read their supporting passages again. Meditate upon these riches that assuredly have the power to set you free.

You're on the downhill side! Good for you! You've trekked through this work, and hopefully, you have discovered some spiritual stepping stones along the way that will provide you some stability and assurance as the turbulent waters of your infertility boil beneath you. Envision yourself as being more than half-way there ... half-way to the lush, tranquil bank where you will be able to look back upon your rampage through infertility and know you made it to the other side. Continue on. There are just three more principles of hope to which I want to lead you. And trust me; their potential to steady your soul can be monumental.

"You've been through hell and half the state of Georgia." I'll never forget these words. It was a statement Rebecca, the other member of my two-member infertility support group, made after my fourth miscarriage. Through hell and half the state of Georgia. You know, for a second I might have thought that was true! (Note to anyone not familiar with God's description of the "real hell": In comparison to eternal damnation, my infertility was a walk in the park. So if your eternal home is not Heaven, please trust Jesus and secure your home in Heaven!) And although, my memories of the reproductive trauma I encountered are no longer as raw and "fresh" as they once were, I still have no doubt about why Rebecca made such a statement. What I had experienced was "a hell" on earth.

The Step Down Room. Go there with me for a moment. What on earth is a Step Down Room? I had never heard the term (nor had any of my family) until my myomectomy procedure. But somehow after this surgery, I found myself groggily waking up in such a room. All I can figure is all of the hospital staff had just attended a continuing education course and learned all about their hospital's new "step down room." Every nurse I saw seemed to be scurrying around, all chipper, tending patients in their "step down room." It was the Word of the Day: "Mrs. Farmer, how you doing? You're now in the Step Down Room." "Come this way, Mr. Farmer. She's in the Step Down Room." "Are you her parents? Oh, she did great and is now in the Step Down Room." "Mrs. Farmer, let's get your blood pressure now that you're in the Step Down Room." "After she uses the restroom, she'll be able to leave the Step Down Room." It was insane! I have no idea how the room got its name, but as the anesthesia began to wear off, I knew I was in the wrong room. I wasn't stepping down. I was stepping off.

The moment I showed any signs of being coherent, my nurse (who had no inside voice) began pouring water down my throat. It was approaching "closing time," and she wanted me to pee and leave NOW! She started with the water. I felt as if I was being water-boarded. She stood right at my bedside, the pink plastic cup with the flexible straw bent towards my mouth. "Come on. Have another sip, hon. If you don't use the bathroom, we'll have to start a catheter." Then it was the Coke. "Well, if you don't feel like you can go, you need to drink this Coke. Do you want a catheter?" I did *not* want a Coke. And what kind of question is that? "Do I want a catheter?" For real, lady. What I wanted was to go to the bathroom so I could get away from this witch!

By the time she came up with the Coke idea, the surgery center was closing down. Nurses, custodians, the receptionists were all leaving for the day. I watched them pass by the foot of my bed with their lunch satchels on their shoulders, cell phones to their ears and car keys in their hands. Heading home. Everyone was heading home except for me and this brazen nurse who was trying to drown me with Coke. It was terrible. The hall lights were being shut off, and I was left with the Step Down demon who constantly kept saying, "Honey, you *have* to drink this Coke. We don't want to have to give you a catheter." Really? I didn't want her to have to give me one either! But I could not pee. My poor mom. She had Dad and Rusty sitting in the hallway offering intercessory prayer. "Just pray she pees! Please, y'all!"

All the while, I am getting sick. The Coke was making me sick. I didn't want a Coke to start with! I told that nurse I did not want a Coke, and now, the Coke that I did not want, was making me sick. I told her repeatedly I was going to be sick. When she let me come up for air in between the mandatory sips, I would remind her. "This Coke is making me sick." And sure enough, it did. "I told you so." I puked everywhere. Coke-Puke was everywhere. In the bed. In the garbage can (which Rusty was holding). In the remote that calls the nurse. In the Coke – which at this point I had almost finished.

Eventually I peed. I have no idea what time we got out of that clinic. It was way past hours, and my nurse who wanted so desperately to "fly the coupe" was left to clean up a huge mess. But I peed! Hell and half the state of Georgia? No. Not quite that far! Maybe just through Macomb County though.

I know you are all-too-familiar with the ruthless ride of infertility. At some point, we feel we have been through all the condition has to offer, and then we encounter some new misfortune that we had never expected to face. Whether it was the discomfort of a medical procedure, the heartache of "another let-down," or the anxiety that comes with waiting for a test result, we have all begun our own excursions that have led us to Georgia's state line.

My Step Down Room experience certainly qualified as a brutal "landmark" on my infertility journey. It was a physical impasse for me – for the most part, only my tangible, fleshly body was victimized that day. But, many of the other notable milestones along the way proved to render vicious blows to my heart. Such was the stowing away of "my box." For more than a decade of my married life, I had accumulated a fairly substantial collection of baby hopefuls. You know how we prospective mothers-to-be do. We fantasize about our life as a mother, our baby, his/her nursery, his/her wardrobe. We reluctantly, yet expectantly, dream about the day we rock our nursing, long-awaited gift, while singing sweet lullabies of the faith in the quietness of a picture-perfect nursery. And over the course of time, we acquire – we acquire, oh, you know, little odds-and-ends that will all be a part of the glorious reality.

I knew it had to be done. Upon being scheduled for the partial hysterectomy that would bring an absolute end to my maternal aspirations, I had approximately three-and-a-half weeks to try to troubleshoot the situation. I had to mentally project myself into the future and then attempt to eliminate the factors that had the potential to drive me to a possible breakdown. I knew I had to pack my box. I had thought about it early on, right after the surgery had

> At some point, we feel we have been through all the condition has to offer, and then we encounter some new misfortune that we had never expected to face.

been scheduled, but I said nothing to anyone. I got my house in order, stocked the kitchen with a good supply of groceries, arranged for substitute teachers at church, altered my work schedule, and I even made my rounds to all my sweet grandparents (just in case something went wrong – know what I mean?). But I put off "packing my box." Finally one day, I told Mom I needed for her to come over and help me box up a few things that I needed to get out of the house.

For years each time I opened the cabinet under our bathroom sink to grab a towel, I'd see an unused ovulation predictor kit. Each morning as I would search through our closet for something to wear, I'd spot the adorable take-me-home outfits I had bought for little baby Farmer. On Saturdays as I'd rummage through our bookcase in pursuit of a commentary for a Life Group lesson, I'd notice the collection of "Now That You Are Pregnant" books. And every now and then I'd make it upstairs to our overflow closet where I'd come across a maternity top or two – pressed and ready to be worn. It all had to go! I knew that if I came home – without a uterus – to a houseful of reminders of my defeated dreams I would not make it. Even if I just visually "bumped" into these souvenirs of my reproductive expectations, it would be too much for me.

Mom came over. And I (we) covered quite a bit of ground that day in the Hades-Georgian expedition. Piece by piece, I rounded up the "baby stuff," and Mom packed it away. Apart from Rusty, no one knew my collection existed. I was glad Mom got to see the pink-gingham, ruffled jumper. We have the same taste; I knew she'd love it. I wonder ... Have I ever been as sad in my life? It was as if I was burying myself, my dreams, my future all into a Rubbermaid chest and then sending them off to a place of safety, but away from me, to my parent's attic. Although I'd never need my box, I still wanted it.

Listen to the Apostle Paul as he describes his New Testament ministry. He recognized that his testimony, which is included in his letter to the Corinthian church, could lead some to suspect a slight case of insanity.

"I am talking like a madman – with far greater labors, far more imprisonments, with countless beatings, and often near death. Five times I received at the hands of the Jews the forty lashes less one. Three times I was beaten with rods. Once I was stoned. Three times I was shipwrecked; a night and a day I was adrift at sea; on frequent journeys, in danger from rivers, danger from robbers, danger from my own people, danger from Gentiles, danger in the city, danger in the wilderness, danger at sea, danger from false brothers; in toil and hardship, through many a sleepless night, in hunger and thirst, often without food, in cold and exposure. And, apart, from other things, there is the daily pressure on me of my anxiety for all the churches." II Corinthians 11:23-28[1]

Are you really getting this? Consider the quality of life for the apostle whose ministry "rocked our world" for the sake of Christ. Did you get all of that? Don't just skim over the "Recent Events" section of his ministry newsletter. Take a few minutes to really mull over these ministry happenings. In jail – that did not include intramural sports, daily work-outs at the gym and a few "smokes" in the general population's courtyard. Then the beatings. That's hard for us to even imagine. I'd venture to say few – if any – of the readers of this book have endured a short-lived fist fight, much less countless beatings with multiple lashes. Shipwrecked and adrift at sea ... to me, that did not involve an inflatable raft or a personal floatation device. Just think of that. Treading turbulent, man-swallowing-fish-infested waters for a day and then into a starless night. That survival story alone would grab the attention of today's Hollywood film makers. And then imagine living your life trying to escape a human predator who is constantly close on your heels. That could be the worst. We've all had the nightmare in which we are running from the "bad guy." It is always miserable, and our sudden awakening leaves us with a racing heart and sweat-soaked sheets. No food. No coat. No sleep. For Paul, it had to be a life of complete agony. He wasn't only tormented physically; his mental and emotional toiling should also be considered. He was the object of hate. Loneliness must have plagued him. Relentlessly, his mission seemed to be one of failure. With no reservations, we can agree that, figuratively speaking, the Apostle Paul had spent at least a day or two on the byways of the Great Peach State.

Chapter XIII

Principle Five: Embrace the Keys to True Contentment

It was during a Wednesday night student Bible study when God used the Second Corinthian account of Paul to convict my downhearted, yet sinful, spirit. As I read Paul's testimony, I couldn't help but think, *Wow! Someone out there has it worse than me!* Even though I was still dealing with the aftermath of the fourth miscarriage, I still had no case for trying to prove within my intellect that what I had experienced was comparable to the hardships of Paul. It was no match. Paul won. Hands-down. The Step Down Room. The two-night, non-bladder-voiding-stay in the hospital. The emotional rollercoaster which I was forced to ride and re-ride for twelve years. The severed heart over remaining childless. And even the ER episode to ease my excruciating cramping caused by a uterine catheter (which by the way, could have resulted in some jail time for Rusty being that he was threatening to flip over the two-seater BMW which was parked in Physician Parking – the car he assumed to be my endocrinologist's). *All* of it considered and tallied up. Still Paul won. His trials surmounted mine from every angle.

At first I was convicted over my attitude toward my fertility calamities. For months, I had deemed myself to be a recipient of some of life's greatest tragedies. And then with a close, intentional look at *poor* Paul, I quickly renounced my negative assumption. Truly, the apostle had endured more, much more. Oh, and by the way, his sufferings were all somehow related to his attempt to serve the Lord.

Our student groups continued to study the passage, and within moments of God humbling me over my "woe is me" outlook, His Word spoke again – loud and clear – to my repentant heart. Paul continues his dissertation of suffering, and then he begins to relate to his readers another ailment, "a thorn in his side." As he concludes his reference to his thorn, his tune begins to change. Paul begins to reveal his true source of joy – the joy which will become the subject of his Philippian letter which he goes on to pen some six years later.

After pleading with the Lord three times for a removal of the thorn (perhaps a physical problem, perhaps not), Paul hears the Lord say these life-altering words, **"My grace is sufficient for you, for my power is made perfect in weakness."**[1] In his downtrodden condition, the Apostle Paul prayed – crawling before the Lord's throne and begging the Lord God Almighty to take the pain away, to take the pain away, to *please* take the pain away. And the outcome was the above statement. No tweezers. No disinfected sewing needle. No thorn-removal for Paul. Instead, a promise from the God of the Universe was granted to the ailing missionary. And it worked! The exact fail-proof remedy that Paul needed was prescribed by mankind's Manufacturer. And Paul got "fixed."

So, what is it about this two-fold promise that offered to Paul hope for his hopeless situation? What is the "magic" (a.k.a. God-doing) behind these words? Paul was promised (1.) a sufficient amount of God's grace, and (2.) God's power would be fulfilled. And with that guarantee, Paul was not only able to cope, but he was also able to find true joy and contentment.

So, let's look carefully at this sacred vow of the Lord. We've already identified that our toiling with infertility becomes somewhat insignificant in light of the hardships Paul encountered. Now we are witnessing (via Paul's ministry newsletter), a promise of the Lord God as it fully heals a suffering believer to a state of gladness and satisfaction. With these considerations in mind – (a.) our trials are no greater than Paul's trials, and (b.) God's assurance for Paul proved successful – we can quickly recognize that this same Second Corinthian promise of God is certainly able to rescue us, the infertile, from our bleak circumstances.

God ordained for Paul to keep his thorn, but with a condition: God was sending a sufficient dose of His grace. Grace is derived from the Greek work *charis*, and when researched, we discover this definition: God's benefit and favor.[2] Just think of that for a moment. A loving Abba Father was assuring Paul, His struggling child, that His *favor and benefits* would be poured upon his life. The Lord made a supernatural pledge with Paul – regardless of his circumstances (whether they changed or not), the holy, righteous, gracious favor of Himself would prevail in Paul's life. And the amount was also disclosed. Not just a smidgen of His benefits. Not just a day's supply of His favor. Not just a week's worth of His grace. But God Almighty, our loving spiritual Daddy, promised Paul *enough* grace. That is grace enough to satisfy, to suffice. His grace would be plenty.

The second aspect of God's oath was given. The Lord continued His vow with a promise that His power (also translated as *the miraculous, mighty work of God*)[3] would be fulfilled. Within the life of Paul, God would complete His work that would demonstrate His miraculous power and abundant ability. With the thorn still lodged beneath layers of Paul's tender skin, God was guaranteeing to somehow perform an extraordinary work within the apostle. In essence, Paul's life was being chosen by the Lord to be the avenue by which the world (from the first century throughout all time) could behold a marvelous, astonishing work that only God could receive the credit for completing. What a package!

> Whatever the future holds — whether you must keep your thorn or whether God Almighty removes your festering ailment — your only hope is to willingly abandon yourself to the Great Physician's antidote.

Paul was getting to be the recipient of an abundant amount of God's favor and benefits. Plus, through Paul's life, the Lord would finish some miracle which would display His power, His amazing ability and abundance. Paul willingly and quickly bared the naked arm of his spirit; the curing injection was administered; and an instant relief came upon him. He received the grace and power of the Lord.

That "shot to the arm" is just what you and I need. Our circumstances are a bit depressing, and there may be no promise from the

Lord that our warring with infertility will end. God may choose for you to endure several more months, maybe even years of reproductive disappointments. You may have box after box of negative pregnancy tests to hopelessly discard. The next six months may account for your household losing thousands of dollars to unsuccessful IVF's. You may still be childless by your dreaded fortieth birthday. And who knows ... your journey through infertility may contain an endless corridor of closed doors, and all you are able to hear from the Lord is a resounding "no." Whatever the future holds – whether you must keep your thorn or whether God Almighty removes your festering ailment – your only hope is to willingly abandon yourself to the Great Physician's antidote. Choose to live within the blessing of all blessings, God's Second Corinthians 12:9 promise: **"My grace is sufficient for you, for my power is made perfect in weakness."**

The disease may never be destroyed. But the potential for it to be harmlessly contained and the promise for a full recovery of joy and contentment are available to you today. I challenge you to go before the Lord, and accept this measure of mercy upon your life. Sit with Him for as long as you need and allow Him to fully grant the pledge of grace and power upon your life. Talk through the future with Your Heavenly Father. As painful as the moment may be, speculate with Him your future with your un-removed thorn. And then, recklessly surrender that future to Him. Hold nothing back from His perfect plan. Relinquish *your* agenda for *His* agenda. That is tough. A complete submission of our desires and plans is not natural; the flesh (our human nature) isn't designed for such abandonment. But do attempt to present yourself, your circumstance, your aspirations, your future – one with or without a baby – to the gracious Shepherd of your heart.

Then avail all you are to be a receiver of His promise. Open up your life to His abundant, sufficient favor, benefit and grace. Only with it, will you ever be satisfied. Then give the Lord permission – not that He really needs it – to make His power perfected (fulfilled) within your weakness. Give Him your battle with infertility. Offer all of your heartache up to your Loving Father and allow Him to use it as the platform by which He completes (finishes) His miraculous work. How beautiful and healing it is when we get to a place spiritually where we can sincerely offer to the Lord our infertility, for Him to utilize it as an arena upon which He can pour out His satisfying grace and fulfill a miracle.

> How beautiful and healing it is when we get to a place spiritually where we can sincerely offer to the Lord our infertility, for Him to utilize it as an arena upon which He can pour out His satisfying grace and fulfill a miracle...

Make your "State of Georgia journey" available to Him. His sufficient grace and perfected power within your life will bring about a supernatural joy ... a joy no baby is ever promised to bring.

Paul stood in line for the life-giving booster, and the impact was immediate. Accepting the "Grace-Power" remedy was all he needed for the uncertainty that awaited him. The effects were instantaneous and wondrous. And there is no reason, my sister, why the same spiritual outcome cannot be yours. Rejoice along with the recovering apostle! **"Therefore I will boast all the more gladly of my weaknesses, so that the power** of Christ may rest upon me. For the sake of Christ, then, I am content with weaknesses, insults, hardships, persecutions and calamities. For when I am weak, then I am strong." II Corinthians 12:9-10[4]

"Therefore" in Scripture simply means "based upon what has just been stated." So, when Paul begins his declaration with *therefore*, he is relating the truth of God's previously stated promise of grace and power to his current conclusion. Paul is prefacing his testimony of being content with the cause or source of his contentment. As a result of Paul receiving God's sufficient grace and perfected power, his heart pledges to boast (or as the original language denotes *to glory or rejoice*) and to find contentment while dealing with many of life's difficulties.[5] With his thorn still agitating his daily existence, Paul was rejoicing **"all the more gladly"** of his weakened condition.

How was he able to look past the pain, the turmoil, and still find reason for rejoicing? His straightforward answer makes sense. He wasn't just okay with his circumstance; he was joyful and glad about it. Why? Because the power, the miraculous strength of a mighty, wonderful work of God, was resting, abiding, "tenting upon" him.[6] Examine the original word for *power* used in the latter part of verse nine. One meaning for the word, *dunamis,* is *a miracle in itself.*[7] No wonder Paul was **"boasting all the more."** He had been granted a miracle, a miracle in and of itself. When the Lord decreed for Paul *not* be to "thorn-free," He supernaturally placed Paul beneath His abundant strength (in actuality,

His sufficient grace and perfected power within your life will bring about a supernatural joy ... a joy no baby is ever promised to bring.

His *miracle*), providing him with an indwelling of *all* he would ever need.

And Paul was thrilled with the "trade-off." He'd keep his weaknesses, his insults, his hardships, his persecutions, his calamities. He'd keep them all. Thank you very much! Because the Divine dividend was so much better. With his thorn in place and with his original prayer remaining unanswered, Paul was getting to *have upon and within* his life God's miraculous power. When the situations that our earthly minds consider disastrous surrounded Paul, he was **"all the more gladly"**[8] because in his weakness, he was strong. The Greek language from which Paul's statements were derived adds an insightful dimension. Paul was claiming to *take pleasure* in his present state of hardships because when he became *ashtheneo* (translated feeble, diseased, sick or impotent) then he was *dunatos* (capable, mighty, powerful, strong).[9] And he had already identified the source of his strength; it was the perfected power of Christ which was resting upon him. And my friend, that is a good deal.

> We are the recipients of a disappointing circumstance of life, but we are also the beneficiaries of the miracle of God's grace and power.

Let's relate this provision to our infertility, if you will. A calamity has come upon us. And we're not exactly thrilled with its visit. In the depths of each of our hearts, we do not want to be infertile; we'd rather not be going through the reproductive ordeal. An unwanted thorn is constantly irritating our attempts to maintain a happy life of rainbows and lollypops. But along with this trying situation (which we cannot alter in any way), we are given an abundance of God's grace and a promise for His power (*dunamis*: God's miracle) to be fulfilled. We are the recipients of a disappointing circumstance of life, but we are also the beneficiaries of the miracle of God's grace and power. Regardless if we get our baby or not, we get the miracle! You and I are guaranteed a miracle of God. His unexplainable, mystical, sustaining grace and completed power are ours! And the miracle – having the power of God resting upon us – is the most precious, valuable commodity in all of our earthly existence.

I want the miracle of God! You, my sister, and I were created to live within the grace and power of God Almighty. There simply is no life apart from either. I'd rather go to my grave as a childless wife and be living within God's grace and power, than to be the spiritually-empty mother of a houseful of children, toiling through life without the grace and strength of God. The Sovereign Lord of all Lords fashioned you and me to live beneath the blessing of a miracle. And when our encounter with infertility leads us to the spiritual shelter of "God's sufficient grace and perfected power," it is there we will find ourselves "taking pleasure in" our suffering.

It's a radical transformation of the heart, and it requires a completely altered perception within our souls. Our trial, the pain, the thorn is an opportunity for us to personally experience God's sufficient grace, His perfected power. A spiritual revolution within us is imperative. True contentment is not the absence of hardship; we gather that from the candid testimony of Paul. True contentment, for a believer, is living beneath the miracle of God's favor and strength. It is what you and I were made for. And no other component of our days spent upon this planet (even the birth of a healthy baby) can bring about the joy and contentment that comes from a daily confirmation of Christ Himself being upon our lives. That is the miracle. I had to repent. I confessed to the Lord my sinfulness. My attitude had been all wrong. I had allowed my fleshly inhibitions to entrap me into believing the "worst's" of life's situations had befallen me. And I was so wrong. So guilty. The ups and downs, ins and outs of my years as an infertile wife were not nearly as unfortunate as I had perceived them to be.

And I sought God's forgiveness. There, on my bended knee, I bowed my broken heart before the Lord and chose to believe with the same, revolutionized mindset of Paul. I made a choice to accept into my heart a new, transformed perspective of contentment. I asked the Lord to radically change my thinking and then entirely renovate my lifestyle. I accepted my Creator's formula for contentment: God's all-sufficient grace + God's perfecting power = true contentment. (II Corinthians 12:9) As His child, I surrendered to the truth of the conditions that led to my joy and pleasure. With a holy awareness, I recognized the elimination of my infertility and all it entailed was not a source for my "**boasting all the more gladly.**"[10] Created in the image of the Lord, I became amazingly convinced of what would offer me lasting contentment ... and that was availing myself to the opportunity for Christ's miracle to rest upon me. With a contrite heart, which had been lovingly whittled a bit by God's Holy Word, I opened myself to the miracle of God's favor and might. And with that conviction and my response, I made a huge detour on the Georgian highway. And then it wasn't long until I found myself spiritually heading towards "higher ground."

Principle One: Life is from God (and barrenness is too).

Principle Two: The Lord brought infertility into your life for His glory.

Principle Three: The Lord brought infertility into your life for your good.

Principle Four: When facing a crisis of faith, be assured – He is the right Savior!

Principle Five: Embrace the keys to true contentment.

Green Pastures of a Barren Land

Chapter XIV

Edited by the Master: Cut for the Sake of Space

Electronic readers. Downloadable books. A literary paradise for John the Beloved. How frustrating it must have been for the God-inspired writer and pillar of the New Testament! He had all the material – the facts, the eyewitness accounts, the ideas. His composition juices were overflowing. His desk was refurbished to the hilt with a full inkwell and a limitless supply of parchment. But how tragic! There was a shortage of shelf-space. I guess he felt obligated to explain the situation to his groupies. You know some bookworms who stand for hours in lines at their favorite author's book signings; they pre-pay for new releases before the copies make it to local bookstores. Perhaps, such John the Beloved devotees needed an explanation of why there would be no sequel to his Gospel novel. Check out his first work's postlogue.

"And there are also many other things which Jesus did, which if they were written in detail, I suppose that even the world itself would not contain the books that would be written." (John 21:25)[1]

Poor John. He had so much more he wanted to write about, so much more he could have written about – but the "world itself" couldn't shelve his works. Don't you just love that? We gain a pretty cool bit of insight from his John 21:25 disclaimer. There is more to the story! What we read in the Bible is just *part* of the plot ... a minute part of the plot!

Yes, it happened back then, I'm sure. I am certain (especially after considering the above statement of John) that some woman living in either Old Testament or New Testament times encountered incurable barrenness. Yes, that is likely. Although her story goes unrecorded in the #1 best-seller of all times, I am confident that she existed. And more than likely, there was at least another gal or two (or several thousand) who shared the condition of being barren but not by choice or by Divine judgment. Somehow these accounts didn't survive the revision process in the final edit of my Bible.

This was an issue for me. I really believed I could have braved the waters of my realized barrenness with more agility and stamina if I could have opened to the supposed book of *"Priscilla"* and read the memoir of a first-century Christian wife who faced her childlessness with courage and obedience to her Lord. But never was such a literary testimony availed to me within the pages of God's Word. Although my saintly sister-in-infertility "Priscilla" *could* have existed, I've never read of her in my Bible.

We all have encountered certain circumstances to which are not specifically referred in God's Holy Word. Such is the case of a dear man my family has grown to love, Jimmey Griffith. As a raring-to-go, recent college grad, Jimmey was thrilled with his newly-acquired management position at a grain company. He and his wife had purchased their first home and were eager to start their family. Between the two of them, Jimmey and his little bride had a reliable household income, and the couple was enjoying a transition time which allowed them to focus on their careers, strengthen their finances and still take time for the leisure of a newly-wed life. On the weekends and evenings in between, Jimmey found time to fish, hunt, play softball, landscape the yard and cut truckloads of firewood. The Griffiths were simply living the American dream as a happy couple, and all the while, they were active in a local church and were committed to their personal walks with the Lord. Their love for each other and the Lord was a powerful testimony for all to see.

May 11, 1983, should have been an ordinary day at work for Jimmey. But as he swept soybeans in a grain bin at his loading station, he lost his footing and slid helplessly into the spinning auger. Within seconds, Jimmey's left leg was literally eaten by the ruthless machine. The simple, common task of sweeping grain into an auger took from a vibrant, healthy, athletic, strong, and God-fearing man his ability to walk. His life was totally changed in less than 20 seconds. After thirty-plus surgeries, battles with infections and two months in intensive care, doctors finally said Jimmey would be okay. There were many touch-and-go moments during his four-month hospitalization. During mid-September, Jimmey was finally permitted to return to his home in West Tennessee. He then started life all over – adapting to a set of crutches and the horrid phantom pain of his missing leg.

What a tough situation. A man, who loves the Lord, becomes an amputee in the prime of his life. One of the most active "fellas" on the planet had stripped from him his ability to partake in the activities that were such a huge part of his life. His future of dragging monster bucks out of the woods, playing soccer with his daughter, leading his team to the church-league championship was all over. Gone. Gone forever.

Oh, how I bet Jimmey wished he could have looked within the pages of God's sacred book and read of a strapping young Jewish man who had experienced the same loss. Wouldn't the details and prognosis of such a personal account helped Jimmey adjust to his "new" life? Jimmey surely longed for a shared, Biblical "story." And not just Jimmey. Consider his precious wife who spent day and night in a cold, lonely waiting room. Her heart desired for God to address her situation – now as the wife of a disabled man – specifically. She and Jimmey both had based their lives upon God's Word, and I'm sure they would have treasured a passage from the Bible that related directly and specifically to a couple who had faced this type of catastrophic injury. But a couple with a similar play-by-play "story" just could not be found in the God-breathed book.

How about my sweet sister-in-Christ, Amanda? She, too, has endured a hardship not distinctively addressed in the Bible. Her fourth pregnancy began as a wonderful, welcomed opportunity for another "Swisher baby" to be added to the quiver. She and her husband of 12 years eagerly awaited the 20-week, gender-reveal ultrasound.

The couple and their adorable three children had recently moved from Tennessee to Montana in order to serve as missionaries in an area completely deprived of churches. Their move left close-knit, loving families grieving for them on the opposite side of the country. Their relocation required them to live totally by faith – trusting God for every meal, tank of gas, and prescription for a congested toddler. The mission work would begin with them. With a determination for the cause of Christ, they sold most all of their possessions in a yard sale, packed up what little remained and headed to do a great work for God in the Bitterroot Valley.

When news of a fourth baby arrived, they humbly accepted one more mouth to feed as a gracious gift from the Lord they served. Ultrasounds were second nature for Amanda, but the couple still cherished the appointment which had always left them (and now their children) in a state of awe before the Lord. Seeing your baby for the first time never gets to be "old hat," so the Swisher family took advantage of the four-month sonogram which could reveal if it was Baby Sister or Baby Brother on the way. The images quickly revealed it was Owen in Mommy's belly ... not Olivia. And with excitement, their hearts began to welcome his arrival. The day of wonder in the Imaging Department suddenly became not-so-typical for Amanda and her husband. With discretion, the technician (and then doctor) explained that an abnormality had been spotted and further testing would be conducted. A miserable couple and their three naïve children left the clinic that day. And the following months grew grimmer for the missionary family.

Amanda ended up carrying within her for nine, full months, Owen "Roscoe" Swisher. His intra-uterine history was normal. The normal fluttering around four-and-a-half months. Then the gradual pushing on Mommy's side. The hiccups around month seven. And then the violent squirming that sometimes made his carrier a bit self-conscious of her rolling, taunt maternity top. And then on Sunday, September 4, 2011, just as doctors had anticipated, a lifeless (and red-headed) Owen was delivered into a family who could not have loved him any more. He was born with holoprosencaphaly and Trisomy 13, and such conditions were not "compatible with life." Such a sweet baby. So helpless. So innocent. Perfect in every way to his parents, entered and then exited the Swisher household.

I don't get this. And neither do you. That is pain. Pain that is only explainable by the fact that our world is fallen and is under the reign of an evil prince, Satan, himself. And although we are able to read of children dying at birth within the Bible, not much attention is given to the details of the day-in-day-out life for the faithful couple who is called to birth and bury their precious son all within one day. For some reason, God withheld the specifics of such a tragedy from His Holy Book. Perhaps, the momma who leaves the maternity ward with nothing but an empty blanket would have benefited from a Biblical account of the same loss. Perhaps.

And then there is Kris. Kristen Smith Robinson. Kristen knew no life outside of the "glass house." Throughout her childhood, her father had served as pastor of a Baptist church in southern Ohio. She had grown accustomed to the P.K. (Preacher's Kid) persona, and the "happy spot" of this 14-year-old girl's life encompassed her being in the school band, playing a variety of instruments and aspiring to be a varsity cheerleader.

On a chilly November afternoon, Kris and her boyfriend at the time (now husband) were picking corn. For you city gals, with little farming background, this task involves a tractor, drive shaft, grain pan, grain elevator, power take off and a grain wagon. I consider myself somewhat of a country gal. I'm fairly familiar with tractors and wagons, but *drive shaft, grain elevator, power take off and grain pan* had me all confused. Thanks to a mini-presentation complete with a diagram and quite a bit of patience provided by my hubby (who is a true "Farmer" – and not just by surname), I was able to broaden my commercial agriculture knowledge related to this fall-of-the-year farming chore.

Here's my attempt to explain corn-pickin': (Pardon is requested if I sound way too "citified" or girly.) A tractor has coming out the back of it a "power take off." The "power take off" is just a type of machine that connects the rear of the tractor to other implements (in this case, a grain elevator.) Coming out of the power take off mechanism is a long, metal rod that can be about three inches in diameter. This metal rod, known as the drive shaft, is constantly spinning; it is the channel that carries the energy from the tractor to whatever implement is attached to the tractor. You may have seen this metal, turning rod as it operated a bush hog. In this case, the drive shaft rod was connected to a grain elevator. A grain elevator is exactly what you're envisioning – some kind of belt-operated platform that extends up into the air that has the potential of dumping grain into a wagon or grain bin. (Boy, how I hope this is making sense.) So, in light of this corn-pickin' incident involving Kristen and her boyfriend, the teen sweethearts' job was to place ears of corn into a grain pan which would then empty the ears onto an elevator. The ears would then ride up the conveyor belt of the elevator and then spill over into a wagon. All of the energy that was powering the belt of the elevator was coming from the tractor (via the power take off which was connected to the spinning drive shaft which turned the belt). How-dy! I think you got it.

Kristen had been appointed the "left-overs position," and she was walking around the tractor picking up any overlooked ears of corn and throwing them into the elevator pan. At 2:15 p.m., as Kristen bent over to retrieve some corn, as she had done countless times that afternoon, her hair got wrapped within the spinning drive shaft (which as Rusty described to me – "spins a million times a minute"). With no awareness of how it had happened, she was twisted three times into the air and then thrown to the ground. That one moment in time granted Kristen the title of the survivor of the largest scalping known within our nation's medical community. Her entire scalp, her ears, her forehead and her eyelids were completely ripped from her by the engaged shaft. Upon arriving at a local hospital, Kristen began her unexpected and unwanted trek through 21 surgeries which would be considered successful if she could be provided with a permanently bald head.

Kristen's parents, Pastor Wayne and Mrs. Smith were out-of-town. It took several hours for them to be contacted. Finally, they entered the hospital that Pastor Wayne had visited countless times before. As they hurried into the critical care unit, he began to pray the standard prayer he offered each time he enter the ward. For years he had prepared to minister to hurting families within his church's fellowship right there – within the same ward. And now he petitioned the Lord once again as he waited for the staff to let him in. "Lord, give me Your words for this difficult moment." And what a difficult moment that must have been for the humble man of God to behold his precious daughter bandaged beyond recognition, knowing the future that lay ahead for her.

Kristen ended up undergoing a series of skin graphs. Eventually, she received the world's largest, single-piece graph. Her hospital bills were astronomical. Pastor Wayne received a statement that was two times the amount of what he made in one year ... after just three days of Kristen being admitted to the hospital! You can do the math. Kristen didn't get dismissed from the hospital for two-and-half months. And her hairless scalp was not considered to be medically and completely healed until almost 21 years after the accident. And no, that is not a typo.

Circumstances like this make the "In this world you will have trouble"-concept of John 16:33 very convincing. The Bible is clear; hardship will come for believers and unbelievers alike. The detailed life of a scalped adolescent is not recorded in the Holy Book; however, we, Scripture-readers, are given notice that trials (more general in their descriptions) will come.

Green Pastures of a Barren Land

Chapter XV

Principle Six: In All Situations, Especially Those Not Specifically Addressed in the Bible,Trust Him More.

While recuperating in the hospital, Jimmey Griffith did not pick up the Bible distributed by the Gideon's International and find a passage that specifically addressed adapting to a one-legged life. Amanda Swisher wasn't able to go home to an online daily devotional site and read Scriptures of a family losing a son to severe brain and genetic defects. Kristen Robinson did not read in her Senior High Girls' Bible Study passages of a gal brutally scalped. (And along with the mention of Kristen ... her father, Pastor Wayne wasn't able to locate a Biblical reference to an under-paid preacher buried beneath the debt of hundreds of thousands of dollars in medical bills.) Such specific accounts are not found in the Holy Book.

The Bible features several ladies struggling with childlessness, but the specifics of the present circumstances relating to *your* infertility and the biblical accounts of infertility may vary. There certainly are details pertaining to your reproductive failures that are not precisely addressed within the Bible. The advancements of modern-age medicine are to blame, in many cases. But it goes without saying, you and

I are not going to be able to cuddle in our beds after a long day at the geneticist's office and read from the Old or New Testament of an infertile gal who had also been under the care of "Dr. Design A. Baby."

After my hysterectomy, I unintentionally allowed myself to become critically lonely. I had no one in my community to whom I could relate as being permanently barren (except for the lady who sent me the invite to the Barren Woman's Club). No one within my church family. I had no book within my library that addressed the woman rendered childless. And I could not recall any biblical mention of a wife, who, at some point did not get her baby. All I could recollect was Hannah, Sarah, Elizabeth, and Rachel. And in the end, they all got their sweet baby (and many times, several, sweet babies). I quickly began to see myself as the only woman who had to live with her maternal dreams unfulfilled. And to be perfectly honest, as much as I adored and loved the infallible, perfect Word of God, I believed I could have benefited from a "Bible story" of the gal who never got her baby. I supposed I would have loved to have read her story, and without really *knowing* her, been able to have identified myself with a woman of the faith who had been plagued with childlessness.

A battle with infertility normally ends with a child at some point. The stories of most women hoping to become mothers have happy endings. I'm aware that many of this book's readers are currently struggling with infertility, but someday, many of your dreams will be fulfilled with the birth of a baby. Many of you will adopt and have your need to nurture met with a child you love as your "own." The percentage of women (and men) who remain childless, not by choice, throughout their lives is nominal. But I am within that percentage, and I realize that this book is now resting within the hands of several women (and perhaps, even men) who are – as bad as they hate to admit it – coming to terms with the possibility and probability of never getting their baby. It may have been just within the last few months that you are beginning to acknowledge the severity of your reproductive condition, accepting that all future attempts to conceive could likely be futile. You may just be mentally "toying" with the idea that the pessimistic attitude of your doctor may be an accurate and healthy perspective. Perhaps you're at the end, and the question has already been answered for you and your husband – there is never a child in store for you; you are irreversibly barren. And if you are irreversibly barren, then you are, to some degree, lonely. You have very few (if any) women in your life who can relate. You're struggling to find resources designed for the Christian childless wife. And your attempts to locate a Bible account detailing a similar end cannot be found.

My loneliness was holding my spirit as captive. I needed God's Word to come through for me. I had always found just what I needed within the pages of my favorite book, but oh, how I longed to read God's narrative of an incurably barren wife. I desperately craved a message from God's Word that specifically addressed my condition. I had shared with Rusty a time or two. "I can't believe this. I'm never going to have a baby, and I'm the only woman who, in the end, never got her baby. Look at the Bible. All of those women who prayed and wanted a baby finally got theirs." Over the years I had found comfort in the account of Hannah. And no matter how old I got, the "story" of Sarah always assured me. But when the end was in sight and I became barren forever, the descriptions of these ladies' journeys through infertility quickly became *not* my favorite passages to read.

Are you there, dear friend? Have you exhausted all measures to find someone, either a contemporary acquaintance or a first-century Bible character, to whom you could relate? Are you coming up empty handed in your search for a gal portrayed within God's Word as the forever barren wife? Are you a bit disappointed, but would never say it aloud, that God didn't inspire someone to write of "Salome" the childless wife of Galilee? I was. I was alone, and within my carnal, limited thinking, I had convinced myself that without a biblical reference to a completely barren follower of the Lord, I was all the more alone.

Who would have ever thought it would be over a chip and dip tray that the Lord would extend to me – once again – His gracious healing? I had been spiritually wrestling with my non-verbalized "let down" in God's Word. (Please don't get me wrong. I still loved every word of His Holy Book, but I believed, whether accurately or not, that a Bible "story" of the wife who never got her baby could have helped me through the finality.) Rusty and I had been invited to some friends' house to visit with a couple who, months earlier, had moved from our community. It was several weeks after my hysterectomy, and I was fully engulfed in my "Sure do wish God had left me something in the Bible about this"-phase. I wasn't bitter. I wasn't questioning God. I was just aware of my desire for something (or someone) to which I could identify.

I was excited about the night. I adored the old friends who were coming to town, and I looked forward to some fellowship – and the food. Finger foods are my favorites! I was standing at the bar (not a wet bar! We're teetotalers!), munching on a beautiful array of the finest hors d'oeuvres known to man. It was paradise. Chips, meatballs, chips, cheese logs, chips, cocktail wieners, chips, and layered dips. My kind of "come to momma" delicacies! (I've never been much on veggie trays!) As I dove head-first with both hands into the salsa and tortilla tray, a local minister approached from the other side of the bar.

This gentleman is such a tender man, and His ability to share God's remedies for hurting folks has ministered to countless people in our area. He walked up to the chip tray, and with his compassionate spirit, he began to ask how I was doing. He and his wife were well-aware of my recent health issues. As we snacked on chips, it was evident we both were sincerely enjoying the "getting caught up" conversation. I told him it had been rough. He shook his head, and a regretful look in his eyes conveyed his typical, caring nature. He commented on how he and his wife had been praying daily for me. And then I told him it was just so difficult for things to end as they did, and that I sure wished God had put a similar situation in His Word for me. I explained my loneliness and how God's Word never mentioned a forever barren woman of the faith. He nodded, smirked a bit. But never was there any sense of judgment. His expression seemed to say, "Yeah, I can understand that." And then Bro. Wayne spoke to me words that rejuvenated my heart and brought to my faith a concept I had never encountered. Still nodding, he said, "Yeah, but it is in *those* situations, that we just have to trust Him more."

He didn't add a book, chapter and verse reference to his truth. It wasn't a word-for-word citation from the Bible, but the reality behind his statement was completely supported with the principle of God's Word. *In those situations, we just have to trust Him more.* There

167

it is! Yeah, for some reason, God censored from His book the description of the believing woman who never got her baby. He didn't want *that* in His perfect Book. Such an account did not make the cut in the Gospels, the Minor Prophets, or the Pentateuch. The Divine, Master-Author left the "childless forever stories" out of the Bible, and He meant to! And now I knew what my response was supposed to be ... **I was to trust Him more.**

My heart was doing holy flip-flops. I then knew God's intent. When I can see a reason and a plan behind just about any amount of "madness," I'm okay. There never was meant to be a reference to a bloody, grain-auger accident, the Trisomy 13 disorder, or a permanently bald preacher's kid in the Bible. There were no instructions for those situations apart from "Trust the Lord more." What a remarkable awakening for my soul! God wasn't being neglectful, forgetful or thoughtless when He left out "Salome's" account of reproductive disappointment. He certainly wasn't being cruel. He knew what He was doing all the while.

When the papyrus parchment was being stained with the ink of men whose very inscriptions were inspired by the Sovereign God of the Ages, the Lord foreknew the devastating slip caused by misplaced kernels of grain that would leave an aspiring young man on crutches for the rest of his life. God foreknew the faulty genes that would cause Amanda Swisher to leave Community Medical Center with empty arms and a broken heart. God foreknew the tragic events of November 4, 1989, that would destine Kristen Smith Robinson totally scalped at the tender age of 14. God foreknew it all. And as He breathed His words into the hearts of the approximate 40 men who penned His book, He omitted the events that with which, perhaps, you and I could have fully identified.

It is our time, my friend, and seeing the benefit is so simple now. So, what are we to do when our reproductive complications bring into our lives situations that are not directly addressed within God's Word? We must trust Him more. We must completely immerse ourselves within the things of the Lord, knowing that the timeless principles of God's Word apply to any and all of our 21st century experiences.

Whatever your state may be in your issues of infertility, if it is or if it is not a topic mentioned within God's Word, trust your Creator and the Lord over your life. Over and over again, place before yourself opportunities to expose your heart to the presence of the Lord and His eternal, unchanging Word. There is an answer to your every question (regardless how contemporary it may seem to be) within the ever-relevant principles recorded within the Word of God. You may never read the specifics of an ectopic pregnancy or the details of an early-trimester miscarriage within the Scriptures, but you will find within the fundamentals of His Word an abundance of comfort and guidance

> Over and over again, place before yourself opportunities to expose your heart to the presence of the Lord and His eternal, unchanging Word.

for all of your daily needs. Lying upon the pages of God's sacred book are endless principles that – although they may not contain references to your particular heartache – have the power to miraculously be applied to your infertile state (whatever it may be). So, I beg you. Saturate your soul with the healing offered by the Lord. Embrace the Scriptures. Engross yourself in Bible study. Obtain the support of your Christian community. Seek out Biblical counseling. And whatever you do, don't fall for the Satanic lie that almost kept me from uncovering my healing. The idea that a Spiritual mentor, whether a pastor, or counselor, must have personally experienced your particular adversity in order to minister to you is not true. **Second Corinthians 1:3-4** promises that God is a **"God of all comfort,"** and it is *He* **"who comforts us in all our afflictions."**[1] I am so glad I did not allow the fact that my Biblical counselors were not on a first name basis with infertility keep me from scheduling my initial appointment. The riches I gained through seeking Biblical counsel are countless, and God used a man and woman who never personally faced infertility to direct me to His truths. And my soul found restoration. That is the power of God's Word.

His Words are life regardless of the situation. Heed the very words of God as spoken by King Solomon, the wisest man of all times: **"My son, attend to my words; incline thine ear unto my sayings. Let them not depart from thine eyes; keep them in the midst of thine heart. For they are life unto those that find them, and health to all their flesh."** (Proverbs 4:20-22) As you walk through your childless journey, claim the strength of Scriptures. **"My soul melteth for heaviness: strengthen thou me according to thy word."** (Psalms 119:28) When your IVF specialist needs an answer *now* and when your heart seems stripped of any peace as you are awaiting test results, cling to the Lord and His promises. Truly, "light" and direction are found in His Word. **"As he spake by the mouth of his holy prophets, which have since the world began ... To give light to them that sit in darkness and in the shadow of death, to guide our feet into the way of peace."** (Luke 1:70, 79)

Whatever you face – uncertainty, isolation, grief, confusion, whatever – trust your Heavenly Father. If His Word specifically speaks of your exact trial, trust Him. And if you cannot find a biblical reference to your particular situation, trust Him. Trust Him, my dear sister. Trust Him more!

> Whatever you face – uncertainty, isolation, grief, confusion, whatever – trust your Heavenly Father.

And I don't know if you recognized the source from which the "Trust Him More Truth" was spoken ... The Bro. Wayne? Yes, that is Pastor Wayne, the former pastor from Ohio, who stood (without a word from the Lord) at the foot of his scalped daughter's bed in a critical care unit only to hear her say, "Yea, Daddy, before you got here, I was just thanking the Lord that He let me live and that it didn't hurt any more than it did." As Bro. Wayne Smith shared with me that evening over a chip and dip tray, surely he knew first-hand the truth behind it all – *In those situations, we just have to trust Him more.*

Principle One: Life is from God (and barrenness is too).

Principle Two: The Lord brought infertility into your life for His glory.

Principle Three: The Lord brought infertility into your life for your good.

Principle Four: When facing a crisis of faith, be assured – He is the right Savior!

Principle Five: Embrace the keys to true contentment.

Principle Six: In all situations, especially those not specifically addressed in the Bible, trust Him more.

Chapter XVI

Principle Seven: *Set* Your Mind on Things Above

I'm so proud of you! The finish line is in sight. You've labored through the pages of this book, and now the ribbon of victory can been seen stretched among the applauding crowd. Not long after the starting gun was fired, you ran upon the first Biblical principle that surely had the potential to terminate you from the race. *Life is from God, and barrenness is too.* But thanks to the grace and mercy of the Lord, you accepted this truth and battled back to the course before you. A much-needed spray of hydration and a sip of water came with the two-fold Divine explanation of principles two and three – *Your infertility is **for His glory** and **for your good.*** Through the bend of back-to-back corners, you powered through the fatigue of doubt and steadied your stride with the fourth truth. *You can forsake your doubt; you **did** place your faith in the right Savior.* The fifth principle attempted to delay your progress, but the timeliness of the downhill stretch pushed you on to record speeds. *Embrace the keys to true contentment.* And now a sure victory is in sight as your body has just plateaued with a refreshed stride after claiming principle six: *In all situations, especially those not* *specifically addressed in the Bible, trust Him more!* And now, one last, crucial, yet perhaps the most rejuvenating expanse of the course lies between you and the waving ribbon of triumph. Don't stop, my sister. Keep the pace. Keep the faith. I want to run alongside you and cheer you on to the final principle which inevitably will sweep you through the tape of victory into the arms of a cheering, exuberant Savior. Your once-crippled heart will be swept up by Him into a circling, jumping frenzy of tears, laughter, relief. Round and round. The Lord Jesus and you. A spinning, ecstatic bear hug. A righteous celebration. The glorious end is near.

It has been almost two years since I became medically unable to have any children. And I can honestly say, I still have not fully adjusted to the reality that I will live my life (whatever of it remains) and then go to my grave as a childless woman. Rusty and I will never be parents. There is not a day that goes by that I do not think – to some degree – about this disappointment. As some of my former students marry and start their families, I am reminded of what "could have been" for Rusty and me. Although my heart overflows with joy, genuine joy, for these sweet couples, my soul aches with regret for the days gone by and the lack of a happy reproductive outcome. For years, as other expecting gals in our family shared their favorite "boy names" and "girl names," I would cringe until the list confirmed that our favorite baby names weren't being used and were still ours for the taking. Now the name listing tension subsides within a split-second when my conscious reminds me that the once-familiar anxiety of "losing our name" is needless at this point. I had always intended to participate in a Bible heirloom plan when I became a mother. This idea would involve me using a particular Bible for about five years, marking key scriptures, taking notes in its margin, writing personal messages among the passages and then passing this Bible onto my son or daughter. Now my 20-year-old, tattered Bible is filled with my colorful symbols and notes, and I cannot figure out to whom the Lord would have me pass it on.

The adjustment to a future with no children is a continual, daily process for me. And I really believe, as long as the Lord has me on this planet, I will be "working through" the loss of my four precious babies and the crushed dream of becoming a mother. A major aspect of my "working through" efforts involves me consciously considering and reconsidering the Bible-based principles outlined in this book. I remind myself of the Lord's Sovereignty, His role in bringing the infertility into my life, and His Divine purposes. I choose to crucify any doubts of His gracious and merciful nature. I spiritually review His sources of true contentment, and I am learning to trust Him more than ever before. At any point and time, I could fall helplessly into the pit of bitterness and self-pity, but I want more for myself. I truly want to live with hope, and with that desire as my motivation, I have accepted and implemented this final principle into my daily existence. And oh, the joy that floods my soul!

"Set your mind on things that are above, not on things that are on the earth." Colossians 3:2[1]

Principle seven is set your mind on the things that are above. Hooray! Doesn't that sound like fun, my friend? Through designing and formulating this book, I have eagerly anticipated elaborating upon this final truth. It is with sheer excitement and a giddy pleasure that I turn my thoughts to the things that are above. There is never

There is never a brighter spot within my day than when I actively set my mind on the Heavenly things.

a brighter spot within my day than when I actively set my mind on the Heavenly things.

When we consider the Greek connotations related to this phrase, we can gain a better understanding of exactly what the Lord intended when He prodded Paul to record this command. "Set" involves a deliberate action on our part and can be compared to the action taken when "setting" a compass. Have you ever been lost? I'm talking about *really* lost? Losing your sense of direction as you drive through a new neighborhood doesn't count. With our modern-day cars equipped with GPS's, Bluetooth communication systems and On-Star, not knowing where you are while driving is *not* really being lost. But being lost, completely unaware of your location and the method by which to find yourself in some familiar area, perhaps in the woods ... now *that* is lost. Just glancing at a cell phone can reassure us when we are perplexed by our "where-abouts" in an unfamiliar town. And so is the calmness that comes over the lost outdoorsman as his hand feels the compass at the bottom of his backpack. By *setting* this tiny, hand-held directional tool, relief can be restored to any off-course woodsman. Upon utilizing a compass, he is no longer lost. And I've never known of a case where a compass failed its user. (One exception as related by Rusty: A compass may not work if used in an aluminum boat.) Compasses simply are fail-proof if used properly by a disoriented sojourner.

It goes without saying that your reproductive disappointments have instilled within you a feeling of being lost, at least from time to time. The "sense of direction" that you once had for your life has become distorted, and now you may be totally baffled by the question of where to go next. You may be emotionally misplaced, and the years of treatment may have left your spirit wandering in circles. The past decade of your life may be an era of you wringing your hands, shaking your head, and being completely bewildered by suggestions and options that have all proven aimless. If *you,* who you are, who you used to be, has gotten "lost" through all of the fertility madness, then I plead with you – Grab the compass of your heart and *set* it towards the things of heaven. That, my friend, is your sure-to-succeed solution! Actively and purposefully, take your thoughts, make them your captive, direct them and re-direct them to thinking upon Heaven. (II Corinthians 10:5) The Greek reference of the Colossians 3:2 phrase is "Turn your thoughts to *savor* the things which are above."[2] After a 12-year brawl with infertility and pregnancy loss, my only hope for a right mind lies within my choosing to let my mind savor Heavenly thoughts. And just like a compass, the strategy is fail-proof. Never has a thought turned toward Heaven not been able to chase away any cloud of regret and sorrow within my soul. So, join me now, dear friend, as we lose ourselves (at least our infertile "selves") within the bliss of some hopeful, healing, Heavenly thoughts.

> Grab the compass of your heart and set it towards the things of heaven.

Linda and Wally married a bit later in life; she was 33 and he was 36. By the time the love-stricken couple said their "I do's," they knew they wanted to immediately broaden their family tree. But after a year-and-a-half of incorporating no birth control, Linda was growing concerned about her failure to conceive. She sought an infertility specialist and underwent a laparoscopic procedure to identify the problem area and "clean up" what could be preventing fertilization. Sure enough, within just a month after the fairly-noninvasive surgery, Linda was elated to discover she was pregnant. The surgery was successful, and the hopeful couple was so excited.

Around week nine, Linda noticed some spotting. Even though the doctors considered it to be mild, she and Wally were very alarmed. An ultrasound was performed, and an ectopic pregnancy was identified. Ectopic (tubal) pregnancies are so very sad. Many times the fearful woman who is carrying a life within her will walk into the Imaging Department of her hospital. She'll undergo an ultrasound and have the beating heart of her son or daughter pointed out to her on a screen. Usually, in the case of an ectopic, a doctor will enter the imaging room and highlight for the shaken patient the dangerous and "unviable" placement of the embryo within a bulging fallopian tube. Within a few moments, the grieving, hopeful mother-to-be will be rolled into a prep suite for a surgery that will remove the child from her body. For Linda, what unnerved her most was the instantaneous nature by which a life could be taken. At one moment, she recalled being pregnant, and then at her next awareness she was back in her room, the surgery was over, and she was not pregnant. Bless you, my sister, if your walk through infertility has led you through the misery and darkness of an ectopic pregnancy.

After their loss, Linda returned home and within a few days, she found herself gathering the tangible memories of this baby. There was a baby picture she hung from their back door for her "I'm pregnant" reveal, some crocheted booties that Wally's mother had made, some ultrasound pictures and other little keepsakes. With no real understanding of what she was doing, Linda boxed up these items and sought to survive the emptiness. Days passed. The "memory box" provided Linda with a sense of acknowledgement for the realness of their baby, but still something was missing for her. The heartbroken novice to the world of pregnancy loss could stand it no longer. She *had* to name her baby.

Linda was serious about the need to give their baby a name. Now, with no "baby on board," she went to the store and purchased a Baby Names book. After searching through endless lists, Linda found the perfect name for their tiny life that never was identified as being a girl or a boy. "Tully" suited either sex, and the meaning was priceless ... "He/She who lives with the peace of the Lord." "Tully" was exactly what Linda's mourning heart needed. She found a resting comfort knowing that her baby (which she and Wally had assumed to be a boy) was living with peace in the presence of the Lord. The couple was assured that Tully was in Heaven with Jesus, living with the peace of God, and they *knew* they would see him someday. "The name" confirmed their belief that didn't need any confirmation, and that being, babies go to heaven. It doesn't take a lot of in-depth Bible study to understand the nature of a God who is **"full of compassion"** (Psalm 86:15; Psalm 111:4; Psalm 145:8; James 5:11)[3] and His role in creating an eternal heaven for babies. After all, in a rebuke to His disciples, it was Christ who said, **"Let the little children come to me and do not hinder them, for to such belongs the kingdom of heaven."** **(Matthew 19:14)**[4] And no one can deny the Providential plan to reunite believing parents with their babies. King David displayed his trust in this truth when he perplexed his friends by cleaning himself up, drying his tears, and going to the temple to worship after his sick infant had died. In reference to his deceased son, King David replied, **"I will go to him, but he will not return to me." (II Samuel 12:23)**[5]

Linda and Wally shared with no one what they had done – the box, the name, the confirmation of their little boy at peace with the Lord. "Tully." They kept it all for just the two of them, vowing to never tell anyone - and figuring no one would understand.

Linda and Wally continued with five more years of infertility treatment and then their miracle (and somewhat of a surprise), John was born. The Lord opened Linda's womb and blessed her and Wally with His hand-crafted gift, all before Linda's forty-first birthday!

It seemed like just a "snap" in time, and 16 years had already passed since little Tully. His big brother, John, was approaching his tween years. And as many families experience, Linda and Wally found themselves smashed in the generational sandwich. Both sets of their parents were aging and facing health issues. And like so many other 50-something couples, Linda and Wally knew they would have to start saying goodbye to their beloved parents.

Wally's father, a.k.a. Dad, was deteriorating physically, and the Deberry family decided his placement in a nursing home would offer him an optimal care that his frail wife of 60-plus years could not provide. Upon being admitted, his health continued to weaken, and his day-to-day activities were minimized to resting in his bed. Dad became less active, less alert and less talkative but more dependent upon the oxygen. Within a year's time of Dad moving into the home, the family was informed that Mr. Deberry's "home-going" was very near. The family would visit him on a regular basis, and they knew each visit could end with what had the potential to become their final farewells.

As the medical staff began to observe Mr. Deberry's turn for the worst, Wally's sister, Marlan, traveled from Michigan to see her dad. Linda was concerned about

Marlan being alone and seeing Dad in such a weakened state. So, in an attempt to provide some support and offer, perhaps, a shoulder to cry on, Linda decided to go with Marlan to the nursing home. The gals' visit consisted of them talking really loudly to a man who seemed to be somewhat misplaced from another time and another place. The girls "fixed" the things around the room that really weren't "un-fixed," arranged and re-arranged Dad's perfectly-placed bedding and then sat aside his bed, patted, rubbed, smiled, remembered – simply loved on the father who had become to his children a dear ol' Dad. It was very evident as the moments passed that he was gradually departing from this earth and entering into the presence of His Savior. In the weeks that had proceeded, Mr. Deberry had, on more than one occasion, faintly whispered the names of loved ones who had gone on before him – often making mention of his father, Pappa D, whose surrender to the Lord called him to be a traveling preacher.

Cautious not to wear Dad out, Linda and Marlan knew they needed to wrap up their visit. They got ready to leave, and as the family had grown accustomed to doing at the conclusion of each visit, they gathered around his bed. Each at his side to caress his lifeless, yet warm hands, kiss his forehead, and tell him once again they would see him soon. As they began their goodbye routine, Mr. Deberry opened his eyes and with sheer resolution and strength said, "Tully sure would have been such a pretty little girl if she hadn't died."

Tully? Linda hadn't even had a chance to think of Tully this particular morning. Tully? The name she and Wally had privately cherished for 16 years. Tully? The name she had heard spoken aloud by just one other person. Tully? And now, coming from the lips of a beloved Dad (who was surely standing at heaven's portals), is the name she and Wally – for 16 years – had associated with their son living in heaven.

Surreal is an understatement for the bed-side moment. First of all, Linda was hearing the *"secret"* name spoken aloud. *It* was *the* name. And to top it all off, *he* is a girl!

Marlan heard her daddy, too. "Tully sure would have been such a pretty little girl if she hadn't died." Linda had a lot of explaining to do when she and Marlan got back to the car that day. The color that left Linda's face, the utter shock that seized her every cell, and the tears that fell generously down her cheeks as she stood aside her dying father-in-law were all deemed normal and appropriate as she told Marlan their "Tully" story.

Truly, the "Tully" account is a Heavenly one. One that I have mentally re-visited time and time again over the years. When God's Word instructs me to "set my mind on things above," I become an obedient child of God as I allow my mind to be taken back to Mr. Deberry's bedside. And I encourage you to do the same. Heaven is real, and for us who have experienced miscarriage, still birth or infant death, our babies *are* there, in Heaven, living with the peace of the Lord. You must embrace this truth, and remind yourself of its reality frequently. I do this with delight. For me, it is not just comforting, but it is (as strange as it may sound) pleasurable for me to entertain thoughts of my four children alive and well in Heaven.

Pregnancy loss and infant death are excruciating, and I just tend to believe that God had upon His heart folks like you and me when He intentionally included the Colossians 3:2 instruction within His Word. In His unsurpassable knowledge, He knew "setting our minds on things above" would be crucial to our ability to live joyful, restored lives. It simply is imperative. We *must* think upon Heaven.

Rusty and I chose to name the babies we lost through miscarriage. Today, they are a part of our family. I've purchased birthstone jewelry in their honor. I've planted spring bulbs to commemorate their lives. We've had lakeside memorial services. My parents purchased a beautiful, iron children's table set with four toddler-sized chairs to memorialize them. And hanging from each chair is a brass label inscribed with each name and "birthdate." As a family, we have actively incorporated our babies' existences, although they be unseen, into our lives. It is our mind-set, and I'm so glad that it is. Just the other day, I came face to face with the "realness" of me being a mother.

In His unsurpassable knowledge, He knew "setting our minds on things above" would be crucial to our ability to live joyful, restored lives. It simply is imperative. We must think upon Heaven.

My dad is undoubtedly my hero of the faith – next to Christ, of course. He is always seeking to use Christ's love to change someone's life. (Or may I say more appropriately? ... He is always allowing God to work through him to touch lives.) Dad and I were on our way to the meat-processing plant with a couple of deer we had harvested, and along the way we stopped and picked up a young fella that Dad has befriended over the years. James had been in jail for several years, and he had lost track of our family. (Notice: Our family hadn't lost track of James; it's easy to keep up with someone when he is incarcerated.) Now that James was out, Dad was trying to help him stay clean and find *legal* methods to make some money here and there. I'd known James for years; as a matter of fact, it was through my undergraduate internship at a local, public housing neighborhood that my family became acquainted with him. So, here the three of us stand at the counter of the meat plant waiting to place a processing order. James and I are chatting, trying to get caught up. I asked about his momma, his twin brother, his kids. He goes through the run-down, and then says, "What 'bout choo, Miss Candise? You 'en Mister Rusty got any kids?" I still do not do well with this question. I ho-hummed a bit, "Naw, we just never did very good with that." And then my 67-year-old dad, honestly the apple of my eye, who was by this time exhibiting signs of wanting a nap (we'd been up since 4:30), abruptly entered the conversation. As he propped up on the counter, he looked at me, and with a tone that said, "But wait. That's not right," he said, "Well ... there's four in heaven."

See there. My dad's got the picture! He has permitted a Heavenly-viewpoint to re-position his earthly thinking to eternal thinking, and now that mindset overflows through every aspect of his life. It was a bit awkward that morning. A white-headed man, his daughter and a 26-year-old convict standing among Polish sausage and jerky, discussing reproduction. Kinda a bit strange. But my dad's compass was pointing the right direction, and oh, how I wish my thoughts were as heavenly-fixed as his!

There is no denying it; if you have ever lost a baby to miscarriage or infant death, you know first-hand the comfort that comes from knowing your child lives in Heaven and that one day you will be reunited with him/her. The promise of Heaven seems to grant to us the hope of finally becoming mothers. I eagerly await my re-location to the celestial city for many reasons. Ultimately, I crave the perfect fellowship with the Lover of my Soul, Jesus Christ, and I long for a flesh-less existence in which I can fully live with no sinful struggles. But I would be lying, if I didn't acknowledge my daily yearning to be with my babies. One of the ultimate aspirations of my life was to be a mother, and I believe with all my heart, I will be able to fully engage in a maternal role upon my entrance into Heaven. My four miscarriages deposited for Rusty and me four children into Heaven. They are waiting there now, and one day we will all be together.

Now, for you ladies who have never (at least to your knowledge) conceived. Please don't let your conniving enemy deceive you into believing that your Heavenly future does not involve being a mother. I've often heard gals say, "Well, I'm so glad that I at least got pregnant" as if conceiving was the only guarantee of a baby awaiting them in Heaven. Where in the Bible can you find a philosophy that indicates an earthly conception is the only method by which a couple can have their own child(ren) in Heaven? How do we, as Bible-believers, become so bold as to stipulate what Heaven will be like based upon our ideals and not the Scriptures? Why is it we tend to ignore the promise of First Corinthians 2:9 concerning Heaven? **"But, as it is written, 'What no eye has seen, nor ear has heard, nor the heart of man imagined, what God has prepared for those who love him - '" I Corinthians 2:9**[6]

How difficult can it be to interpret that particular description of our eternal home? We must wrap our finite minds around the infinite truth. Our eyes have never seen anything like Heaven. We've never heard of anything like Heaven. And here's the kicker for those women who are devastated by the theory they will not have children (even in an ideal heaven) because they could never conceive while living upon the earth ... We have never thought of any state of living that will remotely compare to Heaven – not even in our wildest imaginations. So what is so hard about that? Things, circumstances, events that we've never even mentally processed will be a way of life for us in Heaven. Please don't limit the unfathomable God of this universe. He will have Heaven completely perfect and ready for you. It will be more than you could have ever expected or hoped for – more than your mind could ever imagine. It really doesn't matter if you can't foresee and understand how you will have your own children in Heaven, especially since you never conceived a life on earth. The Bible is clear; what awaits you in Heaven is an eternal life that is beyond all your imaginations.

One of the most influential, contemporary men of God, Dr. Billy Graham, once speculated, "I believe God will prepare everything for our perfect happiness in Heaven – and if it takes my dog being there, I believe he'll be there."[7] Now think about that for a moment. "Our perfect happiness" is not the primary intent of heaven; Scripture plainly reveals that perfect worship of our Lord and Savior is the ultimate outcome. For life in Heaven and life on Earth truly are all about Him. The Lord Jesus Christ, the Lamb of the God who willingly died for the souls of all mankind, is the "star;" He got the lead role, and you and I (and our happiness) are simply not major components of the great, eternal plot. Yes, we *will* be happy in Heaven (especially upon the conclusion of the Great Tribulation), but I am convinced that our main source of happiness will be derived from the reality that we are alive, with our Savior, and perfectly worshipping Him. Even though I don't foresee "our happiness" as being the prominent result of Heaven, I do anticipate that at no time will "our happiness" be more fulfilled and sincere than when we, in a sinless state and embodied with the mind of Christ, are bowing before our Lord and Savior, worshipping Him with purest praise. That reality will be the pinnacle of "our happiness."

Still, in light of Dr. Graham's quote, ... God's Word does not specifically tell us if we *will* or *will not* have our pets in Heaven. However, how can anyone familiar with the impact of Dr. Billy Graham's life of world-wide ministry not value his words? I'm certainly prone to believe what he says, and since the assumption behind his "pets-in-heaven" theory does not contradict what is Scripturally true, my heart eagerly accepts the hope his position can offer for the infertile woman, specifically for the one who has never conceived. If Dr. Graham believes that God arranges for our pet (which has no soul) to be re-united with us in heaven – if that contributes to our happiness – then I readily believe God will have no problem granting the wife, who never conceived, a baby to love and nurture within the realms of Heaven. That's really no big deal for the God I know. You may have the baby you've always wanted, and nowhere in God's Word does He state you had to jump through the hoop of conceiving while you were on earth. What He does say is ... He is preparing Heaven for us at this very moment, and realities that our minds cannot imagine will be awaiting us.[8] If you've never *set* your thoughts in that direction, I encourage you to begin the re-positioning process of your heart now. It really feels good!

Second Corinthians 4:18 states, " ... we look not at the things which are seen, but at the things which are not seen; for the things which are seen

are temporal; but the things which are not seen are eternal."[9] Once again, the Apostle Paul makes mention of a believer's tendency to deliberately perceive his/her earthly life with a heavenly perspective. Within this passage, a challenge is made for you and me to *"take aim, regard, consider, look upon"* the unseen, yet eternal, things.[10] That is to be our nature as believers who are redeemed by Christ's death and destined for everlasting life in Heaven. We are to be characterized by our spiritual inclination to focus upon things we cannot visibly see yet know to be eternal. As Christians we are driven to visualize and ponder a state of glory which we have never beheld.

After my second miscarriage, it seemed I couldn't finalize the grieving process. It was as if my heart was rejecting any sense of closure to our loss. I had been encouraged by "empty cradle" books to commemorate the life of our babies in some way. I remember feeling an overwhelming sense of love for the little "Trisomy 15" boy I had miscarried, and for some reason, I wanted others to recognize that love and experience along with me the full gamut of affection I had for him, our William Paul. My spirit's "default direction" was to look upon what I could not see, and one day while sitting at my keyboard, the Lord gave me this song, a tribute to my (at that time) two babies up in Heaven.

"Babies Up In Heaven"© 2001

It's a song for you; I'll play for you, my babies up in Heaven.
You're on my mind, seems like all the time.
Just can't forget about your life.
There you are, my little girl. Walking down the streets
made of gold.

You're hand-in-hand, with a tiny boy,
who now is able to see.
What can he see?

He sees Jesus in the morning,
the crystal sea at noon.
The afternoon's a walk with Gramps,
and the day is like brand-new.
He smiles and walks without a limp.
But boy, I sure miss you.
So tell me how can such a little life not fade from you?

Each day I think, "What would you be if we
could all just be together?"
Is it long, blonde curls? A freckled nose? Could you sing?
Could you run with the others?
The day will come when the wait is done, and I,
I will be right there to hold you.
I promise a trip down to the shore to play
like all mommas are supposed to.
What will we see?

We'll see Jesus in the morning, the crystal sea at noon.
The afternoon's a walk with Gramps,
and the day is like brand-new.
I smile and know it's coming soon.
But boy, I sure miss you.
So tell me how can such a little life not fade from you?

You're such a little life. A few days I knew you.
But the love I feel inside is so real I can't deny.
So tell me, how can such a little life not fade from you?

It's like a secret life, just you and I,
My babies up in Heaven.

Ooo, Ooo

It helped. Being able to direct my "mind's eye" to glimpses of what I had never actually seen – the promise of Heaven – really helped. Deliberately imagining my eternal future as a happy momma comforted me then, and it still consoles me every day. The relief and solace I experience is contingent upon my willingness to perceive the heavenly, unseen reality. And the same is true for you. Heed the words of the Lord, as recorded by the Apostle Paul. Look upon, focus upon what you cannot see; it is eternal. It is your perfect, endless destiny with God Almighty and Jesus, the Savior of Your Soul.

> Look upon, focus upon what you cannot see; it is eternal. It is your perfect, endless destiny with God Almighty and Jesus, the Savior of Your Soul.

Epitaphs. Have you ever thought about yours? Just what would you like to have engraved upon your headstone or cemetery marker? The one-liner description usually sums up the most obvious aspect of the deceased's life. For the die-hard World War II patriot, the rock may read, *"Loved his country, family and God."* For the faithful couple whose remains rest side-by-side, the granite may read, *"Once wed on earth, Forever united in paradise."* However it reads, in most cases, an epitaph conveys a depiction of the deceased that is best remembered by survivors.

I wonder how the people in my life will best remember me. I wonder ... what is the most familiar, distinctive quality or feature that folks associate with me? If granted just one phrase, how would someone acquainted with me summarize my existence? Have you ever really thought about that? Who are you? Who really are *you* within the eyes of others?

Word gets around; doesn't it? It's amazing how you can have a miscarriage, then a year-and-a-half later go to the grocery store, see someone whose first name you cannot remember, and have them look at you as if you're on your last leg and ask, "How you feeling, honey?" And you **know** what they are talking about! Somehow, sometime, someway – they, too, found out about your loss, and although *months* may have passed, they're still thinking about it. Have you ever walked into some community function, let's say a pageant or ball game, and felt like the entire crowd was looking at you and thinking, *Mercy, just wonder when that gal is ever gonna have a baby?* We tend to pick up on those things; don't we? As women who have dealt with some form of infertility, it seems as if we have a banner above our heads. It follows us wherever we go, and many times to the folks who don't really *know* us – all we become is *"So and So - The poor gal who can't have a baby,"* or *"So and So - No telling how many miscarriages she's had."*

We all have adopted some form of image related to our infertility, whether we wanted to or not. It's true. Even as we enter our doctor's offices, the ladies behind the counter differentiate us from other patients by some distinguishing feature or facet that relates to who we are. You may be the lady that drove five hours for the appointment. Or the 40-plus-year-old who's hopeful for one more baby. Or maybe you're known as the little gal who is impatient, young and has plenty of time to conceive. It's true; many times our infertility and/or pregnancy loss can dominate the impression that others have of us. It is so easy for us to become known (at least to acquaintances) by our infertility.

With this thought in mind – and with our current objective of *"setting"* our thoughts upon Heaven – let us contemplate the accuracy of the "infertile images" others have placed upon us. Many times I've thought about what my life of pregnancy loss and now irreversible barrenness looks like on the outside. I've wondered about how folks perceive the outcome of my reproductive history. Sometimes I suspect it may be viewed as follows: *Oh, there's poor Candise. Bless her heart. She tried so hard to have a baby. And now she's never gonna get one. Guess we can honestly say, her life just didn't turn out like she wanted.* That viewpoint certainly is **not** the image I want associated with me. I hope its nature is far removed from who I am, and its ideology is never considered as a possible epitaph – in any shape, form or fashion – for my resting body. I want to set the record straight for the world. If such a flawed impression is related to who you are, whether you have such an image for yourself or if it is the aura others give to you, it is an erroneous perception. If you are a believer in Christ, please do not go to your grave as a childless woman clinging to the mindset that you just had one life to live and it didn't turn out like you wanted. That would be a tragic ending for anyone. And if you sense that your outward nature indicates that same "one life – didn't end good" existence to others, please institute a "new you" revolution into your life.

> As Christians, our hearts' utmost desire should be for Christ to be glorified throughout every day of our lives.

Most people will reach the end of their lives with some issue that has plagued them with an unresolved disappointment or heartache. Rarely can anyone pass into the afterlife with a genuine sense of every, single aspect of his/her life being trouble-free and totally fulfilling. As Christians, our hearts' utmost desire should be for Christ to be glorified throughout every day of our lives, yet we undeniably experience circumstances that our mortal tendencies consider as "not working out as we would have liked." Such is the case of my biological re-productivity (and yours as well; I'm certain). But the major error of the "only, one life, what a shame, just didn't work out"-mentality is the limited notion of "one life." If we truly let the guarantee of heaven invade our daily thoughts and awareness, then our attitudes of prominence for this earthly life will be drastically minimized. We must deny any pity that we (or others) direct to ourselves by the inaccurate concept of "our life" being altogether a disappointment based upon a substantial calamity. If, for some reason, anyone has characterized me as an unfortunate woman because I had one life to live and I never became a mother, then there must be some clarification.

Here's the problem with the mentality that says, *"Poor me. (Poor you.) I never got my baby; life just didn't turn out like I wanted it to"* – this is not my life! My tentative three-score and ten-year allotment for dwelling on Earth is not *my* life. And if you are a child of God, it is not *your* life either! Everything we have, everything we are is not ours; it all is His. Every grain of sand in the vast Sahara desert, every particle of plankton floating in the Atlantic Ocean's 17,543,940,979,332,434 gallons of water,[11] every star in every galaxy (that includes the estimated 350 billion known galaxies in the "observable universe"),[12] and every breath, the 500 milliliters of air which you and I inhale approximately 14,400 times within a single day[13] – all of it is His! The Bible says, **"For from Him and through Him and to Him are *all* things." (Romans 11:36)**[14] Our lives – from each month to each decade, from each sunrise to each sunset, from one heartbeat to the next – every second that life is within us is indisputably owned by the Sovereign God of this Universe. Our entire existence from our conception within our mothers' wombs until the drawing of our final breath, it all belongs to God Almighty.

I have no life of my own. My life is *His* life. "It is no longer I who live, but Christ who lives in me." (Galatians 2:20)[15] What represents "*my* life" is simply a platform, if you will, upon which the Lord Jesus Christ can live *His* life.

Our lives — from each month to each decade, from each sunrise to each sunset, from one heartbeat to the next — every second that life is within us is indisputably owned by the Sovereign God of this Universe.

"We are afflicted in every way, but not crushed; perplexed, but not despairing; persecuted, but not forsaken, struck down, but not destroyed; always carrying about in the body the dying of Jesus, so that the life of Jesus also may be manifested in our body." (II Corinthians 4:8-10)[16] So, there is one aspect of the "hang-up" I have with the attitude of "my life not turning out as I had hoped." This is not *my* life.

I pray that you have grasped that truth, my friend. "*Your*" life which, by this point, may have become a day-to-day attempt to conceive, carry and birth a child, is not really *your* life. If you have surrendered to the Lordship of Jesus Christ, you have forfeited the ownership of your life. It is a struggle to daily yield all we do, say, and think

– all of who we are – to the Lord, but that sweet relinquish of ourselves is the objective of the Master's Plan. Relief and serenity can be yours when you choose to live within the mindset of *your* life being *God's* life.

There is also another "no, no, no" aspect of the *"life just didn't work out as I had wanted"*-outlook. And it must be pointed out. *Life.* What is *"life"* in this context? Let me share with you a somewhat radical conclusion that the Lord has revealed to me concerning *"life."* I'm not sure if this is exactly how each detail will unfold, but I am sure that by *"setting"* my thoughts towards the eternal, I am completely freed (and encouraged) by the Lord to anticipate the following scenario ...

Candise Moody Farmer's Life (which has already been determined to really not belong to her after all)

I'm not exactly sure how my physical life will end; actually, I have no idea. But I am certain there will be some point in time by which I will transition from a physical state of living here upon the Earth to a full, spiritual state of living within the realms of a real Heaven. And whether that alteration of my life comes with death at an old (or young) age, a fatal accident or the return of Christ, I will experience an ending to this present life and the beginning of an eternal life. Now, I am not precisely certain of the details related to this earthly life-to-Heavenly life occurrence (that is common to all mankind), but if you will, for a moment, step with me into the unseen timeframe of "what could be."

My earthly life as I know it is drawing to its end. Either by a sickness taking over my body, an accident that causes my systems to shut down or (my favored option) the never-ending compassion of the Lord being depleted to a "low" that requires the joyous, rapture of all God's saints to their heavenly home. Whatever the specific circumstance, my physical life approaches its end. I'm not sure if my mental abilities at the time of my death or this transition will allow me to "think through" this inner dialogue, but I foresee it sounding a bit like this ...

> *"Well, I guess it is all over now. I'm done on earth now. Wow! What a ride it has been! God couldn't have started things off any better for me. No one has ever been given a better Mom and Dad than me. They were the greatest. And Jon Paul — what a perfect brother. Thank you, Lord. And how did I ever get to marry Rusty Farmer? God made him for me. I don't think I could have ever loved him any more. My family. My Grandparents. My sweet nephews and nieces. Man, I hit the jack-pot! All of the precious folks in my life, all a part of me by the shed blood of Christ. Living on Earth has been great! I've loved all the Lord created, enjoyed a healthy body. It's been good. From the moment I was born until now — God's mercy and grace has been poured upon me and my loved ones. I'm so thankful. But this is it. It's over. What I know to be life — struggling with my flesh, not fully being "one" with my Savior — is now coming to an end. I can't imagine the next life being any better. But I can't wait to see. So, goodbye. Farewell. That's enough of this. I'm going to be with Jesus."*

And bam! It's over. The teensy, tiny, speck of time that signifies my one life upon this earth is over. How can I part from it so carelessly? With such a brief, yet completely heartfelt and humble, reflection upon my earthly-spent years? How is it that easy? To just forsake the one life and unhesitatingly enter another life? How will I be able to fearlessly walk away from the one existence I've ever known and never look back? The explanation is unequivocally reliable. Brace yourself, dear friend. The megaphone of liberty and victory is being drawn to my lips ... I can willingly abandon the present in exchange for the eternal because my days spent on this planet **have not really been *life*!**

No, not at all, my friend! Because God's grace (extended to me by Christ's sacrificial death on the cross) is covering my sinfulness, my real life, the life intended for me, has not yet begun! As a child of God, I haven't started living in the full capacity designed for my soul. Once I accepted Christ, my nature was radically transformed, and I became divinely compatible for life lived solely with the Lord in a perfect Heaven. So, as for what I have experienced up until this point ... it has not been life! Not life for me, as a believer and follower of Christ. The ideology of "*life* not working out for me" as an infertile and childless woman is so very flawed; for you see, I haven't lived yet. My state of being on planet Earth is *not* life – at least not for me and others of the faith. I scorn anyone for feeling pity for me because my life will end without a baby. The perspective behind that sentiment is all wrong. Why? Because my existence without a baby (which will be from now until my death or Christ's return) has *not* been *life*. This condition of dwelling upon the earth is not *life*.

With my thoughts *set* in the direction of eternity, I define my *life* with the Scriptures. And if you, precious lady, plan to cope with victory through your infertility and especially the potential of being barren forever, you, too must adopt for yourself a "new" meaning for *life*. As Christians, here is our life: "**. . . life is in His Son."**

(I John 5:11);

"**. . . your life is hidden with Christ in God. When Christ, who is our life, is revealed, then you also will be revealed with Him in glory."**

(Colossians 3:3-4);

"Jesus said to her, 'I am the resurrection and the life; he who believes in me will live. . .'"

(John 11:25);

"In Him was life, and the life was the Light of men."

(John 1:4);

". . . the Spirit gives life."

(II Corinthians 3:6);

". . . as Christ was raised from the dead through the glory of the Father, so we too might walk in the newness of life."

(Romans 6:4)[17]

Feast upon those truths, dear one. Many believers toil through this world and never grasp the true, Biblical definition of *life*. You do not want to be counted within this uninformed and temporal-minded sect. Infertility is vicious, and if for some reason you are "unfortunately" deemed irreversibly barren, your spiritual well-being and emotional stability rest within your choice to believe God's description of *life*. Life is *in* Christ. Your life is *hidden in* Christ. Christ is *our* life. Jesus is *the* life. In *Him* is life. The *Spirit* gives life, and Jesus submitted to His Father's redeeming plan at Calvary to *give us* life. That, my friend, is *life*. My life. And your life.

> In Him is your life, and your life is in Him!

Do you see the trouble of the influence of the mindset that claims "my life just didn't work out as I wanted it to?" It is two-fold: 1.) This existence is not *my* or *your* life, and 2.) What I (we) have experienced upon this earth really is not *life* at all. Sit there a while and let the spigot of God's healing and hopeful mercies of heavenly-thinking pour into your mind and forever wash away the

198

innate processes that consider only what is seen. Praise the faithful Lifter of Your Head. In Him is *your* life, and your life is *in Him*!

My heart's desire is for you, my sister-in-infertility, to bravely embark upon the new territory that has been set before you by your struggles with infertility. Wherever the monster takes you, may you courageously tread. May you have stowed away within a handy compartment of your heart the seven Biblical truths offered in this book. Refresh your spirit with them frequently. Revisit the Scripture passages with a revived passion to hear from the Lord. And keep ever before you the merciful and gracious nature of our Lord and Savior. And at your weakest moment, may you never forget, my dear sister ...

The God – who loves you more than you can comprehend – "is a God of happy endings, so if it is not yet happy, ... then it is not yet the end."[18]

Principle One: Life is from God (and barrenness is too).

Principle Two: The Lord brought infertility into your life for His glory.

Principle Three: The Lord brought infertility into your life for your good.

Principle Four: When facing a crisis of faith, be assured – He is the right Savior!

Principle Five: Embrace the keys to true contentment.

Principle Six: *In all situations, especially those not specifically addressed in the Bible, trust Him more.*

Principle Seven: *Set your mind on things above.*

APPENDIX

God's Plan of Salvation

How exciting, dear friend! Your reproductive hardships have driven you to the pursuit of contentment, and by turning to these resource pages, you are actively imparting to yourself the one and only true source of contentment. It is so very true; until you humbly come to the Lord of this Universe seeking His forgiveness and surrendering to His lordship, your search for hope and joy will be futile. At this very moment, your Maker is drawing you unto Himself, and it is with rejoicing that I present to you the components of becoming a Christian as outlined for us within God's Word.

Let's begin with a brief look at the Ten Commandments. Commandment #9 is "Thou shalt not lie." Have you ever told a lie? Any lie? A white lie? Answer this question for yourself. If you have ever told a single lie – which the majority of folks have – you are a **liar** in light of God's commandments. Commandment #8 is "Thou shalt not steal." Have you ever stolen anything? Perhaps as a child taken something while Mommy wasn't watching from the discount store? Or, what about the purse full of ink pens, stolen unintentionally from the bank's drive thru? If so, if you have ever stolen anything, you are a **thief** when considering the holy standard of God. Commandment #3 is "Thou shalt not take the name of the Lord thy God in vain." Have you ever, maybe in a moment of rage or pain, used the Lord's name as a curse word or word of disgust? If you have to answer affirmatively to this question, you are counted as a **blasphemer** in regard to God's statues. You have just evaluated your standing with God based upon three of the Ten Commandments, and if you have found yourself to be guilty of telling a lie, stealing anything or using God's name in vain, you have incriminated yourself as being a lying, thieving blasphemer in the sight of a holy God. And if you have ever harbored anger in your heart towards another or looked upon someone of the opposite sex with lust, you have broken two more of the Ten Commandments making you an adulterous murderer as defined by Christ Himself. **(Matthew 5:21-22, 27-28)** Now as you assess your righteousness before the Lord (which more than likely includes your lying, thieving, blaspheming, adulterating, murdering past), ponder your state before the Law Maker.

Would you be found guilty or innocent if you were judged by God's standards? Undoubtedly, you are guilty before the Lord. And His fair and just judgment of you would send you to Hell upon your death. The Scripture says, **"For all have sinned and fall short of the glory of God." (Romans 3:23), "For the wages of sin is death ... " Romans 6:23,**[1] **and " ... death passed upon all men, for that all have sinned." Romans 5:12.** "Death" in these passages refers to a spiritual death, involving an eternal separation from God. It is the pronouncement of an eternity in Hell for the guilty.

So, you are in a real mess. You've broken the commandments of God, and the Bible clearly states God's just nature will sentence you to an endless afterlife of death in Hell. And you need some source of salvation to rescue you from the judgment your sinfulness has destined for you. Well, my friend, that saving remedy is available for you. **Romans 6:23b** states, " ... **but the gift of God is eternal life through Jesus Christ our Lord.**" You see, God is offering to you the gift of salvation, a way by which your sins can be forgiven and you can stand as innocent before a righteous God. He graciously provided the means by which your eternal destiny can be re-routed from one of judgment (which you and I obviously deserve) to everlasting life in Heaven. As a fair and just judge, God had to require some restitution for your transgressions. A redemption payment had to be made to render your sins as null and void. According to **Hebrews 9:22**, that atonement required the shedding of blood. (" ... **without shedding of blood there is no forgiveness.**")[2]

The sins that have left you helplessly standing as guilty before God Almighty can be cancelled by His act of compassion. **Romans 5:8 says, "But God commendeth His love toward us, in that while we were yet sinners, Christ died for us."** Out of His love for you, God provided the sacrifice of His dear Son as an atonement for your sins. Jesus Christ became the bearer of your sins' punishment in order for you to experience the forgiveness of the Lord. The sinless Son of God, Jesus, endured a torturous death on a cross as the payment for all humanity's sins.

Please don't let anything stop you from accepting God's salvation. Take courage in His promise, **"For whosoever shall call upon the name of the Lord shall be saved" (Romans 10:13).** No one has ever loved you more. Won't you let today be the day of your salvation, your new birth in Christ? Please begin your walk with Him, and allow Him to make you a child of His.

Salvation is accepting God's gift. Salvation, becoming a Christian, is someone, like you and me, entering into a love relationship with the Creator of this Universe, and salvation is daily acted upon by seeking to maintain that communion. With a broken heart for your sinfulness and with an awareness of your inability to escape your eternal damnation, bow before the Lord and receive His grace upon your life. Repent of your sins by confessing them to the Lord and seek the forgiveness made available by the sacrificial death and resurrection of God's perfect Son. Forsake your sins once and for all. Turn from them and turn to Christ by yielding all you are and all you are going to be to His Lordship. Surrender your life to Him. Make Him your Lord (Boss). The inception of your new life in Christ is only a prayer away. Won't you go to the Lord now in prayer? Right now, talk to the Lord of the Universe ... Confess your sins, believe in Christ's death and resurrection as the only atonement for your sin; seek the Lord's forgiveness; surrender your life to Him, and trust Him as your Lord and Savior. He loves you so.

END NOTES

Introduction
Psalms 23:2 (KJV)
Psalms 113:9 (NASB)

Chapter I
[1] www.fieldhealth.com
[2] en.wikipedia.org/wiki/world_population.

Chapter II
[1] The Scofield Study Bible, New American Standard®. NASB®. Copyright 1995 by The Lockman Foundation.
[2] The Scofield Study Bible, New American Standard®. NASB®. Copyright 1995 by The Lockman Foundation.
[3] The Scofield Study Bible, New American Standard®. NASB®. Copyright 1995 by The Lockman Foundation.
[4] The Scofield Study Bible, New American Standard®. NASB®. Copyright 1995 by The Lockman Foundation.
[5] The Scofield Study Bible, New American Standard®. NASB®. Copyright 1995 by The Lockman Foundation.
[6] The Scofield Study Bible, New American Standard®. NASB®. Copyright 1995 by The Lockman Foundation.
[7] The Scofield Study Bible, New American Standard®. NASB®. Copyright 1995 by The Lockman Foundation.
[8] The Scofield Study Bible, New American Standard®. NASB®. Copyright 1995 by The Lockman Foundation.
[9] The Scofield Study Bible, New American Standard®. NASB®. Copyright 1995 by The Lockman Foundation.
[10] The Scofield Study Bible, New American Standard®. NASB®. Copyright 1995 by The Lockman Foundation.

Chapter IV

[1] The Scofield Study Bible, New American Standard®. NASB®. Copyright 1995 by The Lockman Foundation.

[2] Psalms 139:14

[3] Strong, James, *The New Strong's Exhaustive Concordance of the Bible* (Nashville: Thomas Nelson, 1996) pp. 36, 1484.

[4] Strong, James, *The New Strong's Exhaustive Concordance of the Bible* (Nashville: Thomas Nelson, 1996) pp. 95, 890.

[5] John 9:3, parenthetical, mine.

[6] Psalms 37:23

[7] adam.about.net/reports/000022_2.htm

[8] The Scofield Study Bible, New American Standard®. NASB®. Copyright 1995 by The Lockman Foundation.

Chapter V

[1] *Life Application Bible* (Wheaton: Tyndale House, 1988) p. 1716.

[2] Strong, James, *The New Strong's Exhaustive Concordance of the Bible* (Nashville: Thomas Nelson, 1996) pp. 87, 1483.

[3] The Scofield Study Bible, New American Standard®. NASB®. Copyright 1995 by The Lockman Foundation.

[4] The Scofield Study Bible, New American Standard®. NASB®. Copyright 1995 by The Lockman Foundation.

[5] The Scofield Study Bible, New American Standard®. NASB®. Copyright 1995 by The Lockman Foundation.

[6] The Holy Bible, English Standard Version®, ESV®. Copyright 2001 by Crossway Bibles.

Chapter VII

[1] Mark 11:24

Chapter IX

[1] The Scofield Study Bible, New American Standard®. NASB®. Copyright 1995 by The Lockman Foundation.

[2] www.archives.gov/exhibits/american_originals/titanic.html

[3] The Scofield Study Bible, New American Standard®. NASB®. Copyright 1995 by The Lockman Foundation.

Chapter XI

[1] The Scofield Study Bible, New American Standard®. NASB®. Copyright 1995 by The Lockman Foundation.

[2] Luke 1:18

[3] The Life Application Bible, The Living Bible®. Copyright 1988 by Tyndale House Publishers.

[4] Matthew 11:2

[5] The Holy Bible, English Standard Version®, ESV®. Copyright 2001 by Crossway Bibles.

[6] Matthew 11:9, 11, English Standard Version

[7] Matthew 11:2, paraphrase, mine.

[8] Time frame taken from note of a sermon by Dave Edwards, July 27, 2010. Carlinsville, Illinois.

[9] The Scofield Study Bible, New American Standard®. NASB®. Copyright 1995 by The Lockman Foundation.

[10] Strong, James, *The New Strong's Exhaustive Concordance of the Bible* (Nashville: Thomas Nelson, 1996) pp. 81, 977.
[11] Matthew 11:6. The Living Bible.

Chapter XII
[1] The Holy Bible, English Standard Version®, ESV®. Copyright 2001 by Crossway Bibles.

Chapter XIII
[1] II Corinthians 12:9 *English Standard Version*
[2] Strong, James, *The New Strong's Exhaustive Concordance of the Bible* (Nashville: Thomas Nelson, 1996) pp. 98, 546.
[3] Strong, James, *The New Strong's Exhaustive Concordance of the Bible* (Nashville: Thomas Nelson, 1996) pp. 25, 1057.
[4] The Holy Bible, English Standard Version®, ESV®. Copyright 2001 by Crossway Bibles.
[5] Strong, James, *The New Strong's Exhaustive Concordance of the Bible* (Nashville: Thomas Nelson, 1996) pp. 48, 513
[6] Strong, James, *The New Strong's Exhaustive Concordance of the Bible* (Nashville: Thomas Nelson, 1996) pp. 35, 1126.
[7] Strong, James, *The New Strong's Exhaustive Concordance of the Bible* (Nashville: Thomas Nelson, 1996) pp. 25, 1057.
[8] II Corinthians 12:9-10. English Standard Version.
[9] Strong, James, *The New Strong's Exhaustive Concordance of the Bible* (Nashville: Thomas Nelson, 1996).
[10] II Corinthians 12:9-10. English Standard Version.

Chapter XIV
[1] The Scofield Study Bible, New American Standard®. NASB®. Copyright 1995 by The Lockman Foundation.

Chapter XV
[1] The Holy Bible, English Standard Version®, ESV®. Copyright 2001 by Crossway Bibles.

Chapter XVI
[1] The Scofield Study Bible, New American Standard®. NASB®. Copyright 1995 by The Lockman Foundation.
[2] Strong, James, *The New Strong's Exhaustive Concordance of the Bible* (Nashville: Thomas Nelson, 1996)
[3] The Scofield Study Bible, New American Standard®. NASB®. Copyright 1995 by The Lockman Foundation.
[4] The Holy Bible, English Standard Version®, ESV®. Copyright 2001 by Crossway Bibles.
[5] The Scofield Study Bible, New American Standard®. NASB®. Copyright 1995 by The Lockman Foundation.
[6] The Holy Bible, English Standard Version®, ESV®. Copyright 2001 by Crossway Bibles.
[7] www.brainyquote.com/quotes/keywords/god_9.html
[8] John 14:1-3
[9] The Scofield Study Bible, New American Standard®. NASB®. Copyright 1995 by The Lockman Foundation.
[10] Strong, James, *The New Strong's Exhaustive Concordance of the Bible* (Nashville: Thomas Nelson, 1996) pp. 82, 818.

[11] http://wiki.answers.com.

[12] www.atlasoftheuniverse.com/universe.html.

[13] faculty.stcc.edu/AandP/AP/AP2pages/Units21to23; http://www.chacha.com/question.

[14] The Holy Bible, English Standard Version®, ESV®. Copyright 2001 by Crossway Bibles.

[15] The Holy Bible, English Standard Version®, ESV®. Copyright 2001 by Crossway Bibles.

[16] The Scofield Study Bible, New American Standard®. NASB®. Copyright 1995 by The Lockman Foundation.

[17] The Scofield Study Bible, New American Standard®. NASB®. Copyright 1995 by The Lockman Foundation.

[18] http://ph.news.yahoo.com (Quote of Fr. Carmelo Arada)

Appendix

[1] The Scofield Study Bible, New American Standard®. NASB®. Copyright 1995 by The Lockman Foundation.

[2] The Scofield Study Bible, New American Standard®. NASB®. Copyright 1995 by The Lockman Foundation.

Acknowledgements

With a heart of sincere gratitude, I resolutely acknowledge my Savior and Lord as the inspiration behind this project. Thank you, Sweet Jesus, for loving me, saving me and making me the recipient of your unfathomable mercy and grace. You have my heart forever!

Many folks made significant contributions to this book, and for them I am humbly grateful. Thank you, My Ten Readers – Linda Cathey, Dr. Joe and Gail Davis, Rebecca Griffith, Richard Jordan, Patsy Kemp, Kim Murphey, Pam Walker, Momma and Rusty – for being the guinea pigs. Also, thank you, Mr. John Treace, and Steve and Annie Chapman. As I began to enter the unfamiliar waters of authoring a book, you were the first people I called! And a special "thanks" goes out to Tammy French, Traci Shepherd and Rebecca (Anne) Stewart.

May the Lord richly bless the precious families whose stories of faith are detailed within this book. You unhesitatingly shared your lives for the purpose of glorifying the Lord. May He bless you all.

I also want to thank the super-talented team of Free Church Press and Peter Lumpkins for believing in the ministry of this book. I truly appreciate your support, professionalism, and patience.

There are countless friends and family in Christ who I wish to thank. My life has been made rich beyond measure by each of you. A special thank you to the 911 Prayer Team; you are my sisters. And may God bless the fellowship of New Harmony Baptist. How beautiful is the body of Christ!

I can never adequately thank the Lord for *all* of my dear family.

First and foremost, thank you, Rusty, for wanting to spend your life with me. Next to my salvation and relationship with Jesus, you are the sweetest blessing in my life. I love you more now than ever.

Mom and Dad, I cannot thank you enough for your endless love. You've spent your whole lives loving Jesus, and I want to be like you. I love you more than you can imagine.

Jon Paul (my sidekick forever) and Erin – Your zeal for this book has been such a blessing! I love you like crazy. Thank you for letting me be Aunt C to "duh boyz"; I often wonder, *could I ever love them any more?*

To my Granny and my Grandmomma and Big Daddy – How sweet of the Lord to give me *you!* Thank you for your love and willingness to do absolutely anything for your family. I love, love, love you!

And to the Farmer clan – only the Lord fully knows how very grateful I am for the icing-on-the-cake blessing that I received on September 19, 1992, when I married into your dear, dear family. Thank you, MiMi, Papa, Jody, Beth, Amy, James, Grandmaw – the list goes on! I love you, and I know you love me. And – XXOO to my wonderful nieces and nephews! Your Aunt C is wild about you!

Thank you, Dear Lord, for my loved ones who are with you now. Their impact upon my life will never be forgotten. I live with their memories everyday, and I thank you for Jesus' sacrifice – for through Him, we will all be together soon.

Additional Resources

Depression. Despair. Anxiety. What seems to be driving countless people into extended seasons of hopelessness? Could it be the rampancy of failed dreams? When "things just don't work out," how can you live contentedly with an unwanted reality?

Discover the answers in God's Holy Word!

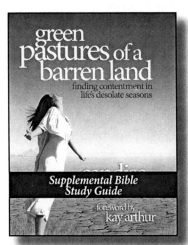

Green Pastures of a Barren Land Supplemental Bible Study

- *8 weeks of study*
- *An uplifting, guided look into Scripture*
- *Opportunity for personal reflection and application*
- *Easy-to-use leader's guide included*
- *An ideal study for the small group setting*
- *Excellent devotional tool for a daily quiet time*

Green Pastures of a Barren Land Companion DVD

Revolutionize your small group Bible study! Sessions feature a brief introductory and wrap-up segment, in which author, Candise Farmer, offers encouragement and insight.
Available online only at:
www.enoughgraceministries.com

Resources by Candise Farmer can be ordered on online at
www.enoughgraceministries.com or www.amazon.com.
Enough Grace Ministries, Inc.
P.O. Box 502
Paris, Tennessee 38242
www.enoughgraceministries.com

CPSIA information can be obtained at www.ICGtesting.com
Printed in the USA
BVOW031257210513

321274BV00001B/1/P